Semantic Web Services for Web Databases

Mourad Ouzzani • Athman Bouguettaya

Semantic Web Services for Web Databases

Foreword by Boualem Benatallah

 Springer

Mourad Ouzzani
Qatar Computing Research Institute
Qatar Foundation
Doha, Qatar
mouzzani@qf.org.qa

Athman Bouguettaya
School of Computer Science
and Information Technology
RMIT University
Melbourne Victoria
Australia
athman.bouguettaya@rmit.edu.au

ISBN 978-1-4899-9807-1   ISBN 978-1-4614-1644-9 (eBook)
DOI 10.1007/978-1-4614-1644-9
Springer New York Dordrecht Heidelberg London

Printed on acid-free paper

Springer is part of Springer Science+Business Media (www.springer.com)

To my parents, my wife, and my children.

Mourad Ouzzani

To my mother.

Athman Bouguettaya

Foreword

The advent of the Web has created a new landscape for the way organizations design and deploy their databases and applications. This has extended the scale of heterogeneity and autonomy of these databases and applications to levels not seen before. Concurrently, a new computing environment is being shaped through advances in service oriented architectures, mashups, and cloud computing. While connectivity is no longer an issue, judiciously organizing web databases and efficiently accessing them are raising a myriad of new research challenges. In particular, it is quite challenging to enable the tasks of finding, accessing, and querying a large number of autonomous and heterogeneous databases which have not been designed to interoperate in such an open environment. Because Web services are increasingly being used as the technology of choice to access Web databases and build applications on the Web, it is imperative to build a new query infrastructure with would enable their deployment and expansion on the Internet, thus providing users with tools to efficiently access and share Web services.

In this excellent book, the authors presented an intuitive and scalable approach to organize and access Web databases. The basic idea is that Web databases can be simply organized based on the different topics related to their content. This creates a distributed ontology of Web databases that are easily explored and queried. Users are provided with tools to find databases of interest to query them without the effort that is usually required in dealing with databases that have been designed and implemented using a disparate set of tools, languages, and systems. The book presents a novel query infrastructure that treats Web services as first-class objects. Queries are evaluated through the invocations of different Web services. Because efficiency plays a central role in such evaluations, the authors propose a query optimization model based on aggregating the quality of Web service (QoWS) parameters of the different Web services involved in the query evaluation. The model adjusts QoWS through a dynamic rating scheme and multilevel matching in which the rating provides an assessment of Web services' behavior. Multilevel matching allows the expansion of the solution space by enabling similar and partial answers.

This book is the first of its kind in providing a thorough treatise of the important problems of deploying databases and applications on the Web, relying on ontologies and Web services as the means to deliver efficient and novel solutions for interoperating Web databases and re-using applications.

Sydney, August 2011   *Boualem Benatallah*

Preface

Organizations all over the world rely on a wide variety of databases to conduct their everyday business. Because of the autonomous nature of these organizations, databases are designed and implemented using a disparate set of tools, languages, and systems. This has led to a proliferation of databases obeying different sets of requirements and sometimes modeling the same situations. There are several reasons that have resulted in the dissimilarity of systems. For instance, some of the reasons stem either from application requirements (business, manufacturing, etc), or technology evolution (hierarchical vs. relational vs. object-oriented etc), or product support (mainframe vs. PC vs. client/server etc). This in effect, created a global system of *autonomous* and *heterogeneous* databases that hardly cooperate to solve common problems. Connectivity of these databases was until the advent of the Web, a major impediment to enabling data sharing of disparate databases. The WWW has solved the age-old problem of connectivity. Any database is now potentially accessible through the Web. However, *interoperation* and *cooperation* have remained *largely* elusive because of fundamental open research problems. The advent of the WWW has in effect brought to the fore the importance of solving this strategic aspect of data sharing.

To allow effective and efficient data sharing on the Web, there is a need for an infrastructure that can support flexible tools for information space organization, communication facilities, information discovery, content description, and assembly of data from heterogeneous sources (conversion of data, reconciliation of incompatible syntax and semantics, integration of distributed information, etc). Old techniques for manipulating these sources are neither appropriate nor efficient. Users must be provided with tools for the logical scalable exploration of such systems. The advent of *Web services* and the area of *Service Computing* around the turn of the century, has provided an impetus for the large scale leveraging of applications. The simple and yet powerful *Service-Oriented Architecture* (SOA) framework has given a second life not only to applications but also databases that were previously hard to access and interoperate with. This book looks at the marriage of the Web, databases, and services to allow the deployment of novel solutions for the easy access and efficient use of applications and databases. The concept of Web databases is defined and explained. An organizational framework for managing Web databases is detailed. Database applications are wrapped as Web services. These are used to transparently access Web databases. A comprehensive query infrastructure for Web services is described. The core of this query infrastructure relates to the efficient delivery of Web services based on the concept of Quality of Web Service.

Doha, Qatar, August 2011   *Mourad Ouzzani*
Melbourne, Australia, August 2011   *Athman Bouguettaya*

Acknowledgements

I would like to thank my family for their unwavering support and help during the preparation of this book: my wife Dalila, and children Hajer, Iman, Abderhamane, Asmaa, and Lina. I would also like to thank my mentor Dr. Ahmed K. Elmagarmid for his continuous support.

Mourad Ouzzani

I would like to acknowledge the contribution of many collaborators who shaped our research in the general area of service computing. I would be remiss if I were not grateful to my beautiful family consisting of my wife Malika, and sons Zakaria, Ayoub, and Mohamed-Islam for their support and understanding.

Athman Bouguettaya

Acronyms

AAA	Area Agencies of Aging
API	Application Programming Interface
FSA	Family and Social Service Administration
IDL	Interface Description Language
QoS	Quality of Service
QoWS	Quality of Web Service
SAW	Simple Additive Weighting
SEP	Service Execution Plan
SOA	Service Oriented Architecture
SOAP	Simple Object Access Protocol
SOC	Service-Oriented Computing
UDDI	Universal Description Discovery and Integration
URI	Uniform Resource Identifier
WS	Web Service
WSDL	Web Service Definition Language
WSMS	Web Service Management System
XML	Extensible Markup Language

Contents

List of Figures

List of Tables

Chapter 1
Introduction

The advent of the Web elicited connectivity to a wealth of information sources and services which had hitherto been inaccessible. Its simple interface was an instant success that helped tremendously in its wide deployment. The early Web provided users access to text-based pages through hypertext links. As the Web evolved (Figure 1.1), its exponential growth has resulted in higher expectations that went largely unfulfilled. Although powerful search engines and data integration systems were developed to sift through the massive amount of information, the ever increasing amount of accessible information has made quality information search an arduous task. The main impediment has been adding *semantics* to the Web so that information can be automatically processed. The envisioned *Semantic Web* aims to fulfill this goal [19]. In simple terms, the *Semantic Web* is an extension of the current Web in which information is given well-defined meaning, better enabling computers and people to work in cooperation [19]. A key player in enabling the *Semantic Web* is the emerging concept of *Web services*. A *Web service* is a set of related functionalities that can be programmatically accessed and manipulated through the Web. Interacting with Web resources, including databases and other information sources, is taking a new direction with the emergence of *Web services*.

Data integration has received considerable attention due to its relevance to a variety of data-management applications and information systems. A large body of database research has been devoted to issues related to building data integration infrastructures. Earlier research dealt with *distributed database systems* [78] *multi-database systems* [23], and *mediators* [95]. In most cases, the focus has been on enabling data sharing amongst a *small* number of databases. The widespread use of the Web has rekindled the issue of data sharing across heterogeneous and autonomous databases. Now that connectivity is no longer an issue, the attention has turned to providing Web-enabled infrastructure that will sustain data sharing among a large number of Web databases. This has paved the way for new research opportunities to provide "*uniform*" or "*integrated*" access to these Web resources. The potential of the added value enabled the emergence of various new Web-based applications. The ultimate goal is to leverage techniques developed in the database arena to the Web.

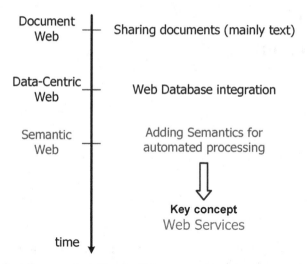

Fig. 1.1 Web Evolution towards the Service Web

This book addresses issues related to the efficient access to Web databases and Web services. We focus on providing a distributed ontology for a meaningful organization of and efficient access to Web databases. We dedicate most of our work on presenting a comprehensive query infrastructure for the emerging concept of Web services. The core of this query infrastructure concerns the efficient delivery of Web services based on the concept of *Quality of Web Service*.

Data management a the Web scale aims at exploiting the immense amount of heterogeneous, fast-evolving data available on the Web. The large number of Web databases greatly complicates *autonomy* and *heterogeneity* issues. This requires better models and tools for describing data semantics and specifying metadata. Techniques for automatic data and metadata extraction and classification (ontologies, for example) are crucial for building tomorrow's Semantic Web [19]. Query languages and query processing and optimization techniques need too be extended to exploit semantic information. Users also need adaptive systems to help them explore the Web and discover interesting data sources that support different query and search paradigms. Data dissemination techniques and notification services must be developed to enable effective data delivery services. Web-centric applications such as e-commerce and digital government applications pose stringent organizational, security, and performance requirements that far exceed what is now possible with traditional database techniques.

One of the most frequently encountered issues in Web databases is how users can efficiently query large and highly intricate amounts of available heterogeneous information sources [75]. A major difficulty in optimizing queries on the Web is that once a query is submitted to a specific information source, control over its execution is no longer possible. Further compounding this problem, that information source may exhibit a different behavior from what has been initially assumed, thus impairing predictions. As a result, traditional optimization techniques that rely heavily on statistical information may hardly be applicable. Query optimization on the Web may also span a larger spectrum of criteria than those in classical cost models. An example is the *information quality* criterion that codifies reliability, availability, and fees. Furthermore, the Web's volatility and highly dynamic nature are a challenge when the expectation is that queries always return results. Also, not all information sources are expected to provide the same *query capabilities*. The query processor needs to make sure that the generated query execution plan is *feasible* with respect to these limitations.

In that respect, we have been investigating research issues on enabling efficient and uniform querying of Web databases. The main focus is on designing a meaningful organization and segmentation of the large information space. This research resulted in an ontology based organization of Web databases or distributed ontology for Web databases [72, 30]. Such organization of Web databases would filter interaction and accelerate searches in the large space of Web databases. Scalability is achieved through the incremental formation and discovery of inter–relationships between Web databases. The information space is organized as information type groups. Each group forms an *ontology* to represent the domain of interest of the related Web databases. Ontologies dynamically clump databases together based on common areas of interest into a single atomic unit. Ontologies are related to each other by inter–ontology relationships. Individual Web databases join and leave the formed ontologies at their own discretion.

We first implemented the above ontological organization in *WebFINDIT* using a healthcare scenario and then in *WebDG*. *WebFINDIT* [72, 24, 26, 25] is a system for describing, locating and accessing Web databases. It offers a Web-centric infrastructure to elicit interoperation of Web databases. WebDG [27, 30] enables citizens to get timely services from local, state, and federal governments. In WebDG, we investigate the design and implementation of a middleware for organizing, accessing, and managing both government databases and services (mostly for social services).

Web services have emerged as an important pillar of the Web revolution and have been used in many applications [91, 42]. Organizations across all spectra are rushing to provide modular applications that can be programmatically accessed through the Web [34]. They are becoming the foundational infrastructure for different forms of dynamic and semantic-aware interactions on the Web. Examples of applications using Web services include e-commerce with all its forms (B2B, B2C, etc.), digital government, wireless applications, and grid computing.

The Web is evolving from a passive medium for publishing data to a more active platform for conducting business. Web services are becoming the *de facto* means to deliver all kind of functionalities on the Web for direct consumption by programs. This is in line with a fully automated Semantic Web where (intelligent) agents would interact with each other on behalf of their owners. This unprecedented proliferation of Web services has been sustained by the intense activity aimed at standardizing different aspects of Web services (e.g., WSDL and WS-CDL [35] for description, SOAP [36] for message exchange, and BPEL4WS [14] for Web services orchestration.) However, it will take much more fundamental research to fully exploit both the *connectivity* provided by the Web and the vast amount of government and business applications that have been developed in the past few decades. Leveraging the Web as a facilitator for efficient delivery of Web services is of paramount significance to a large array of constituencies. Governments would be able to better serve citizens and their other constituencies by streamlining and combining their Web accessible resources. Businesses would be able to dynamically outsource their core functionalities and provide economies of scale.

The ability to efficiently access and share Web services is a critical step towards the full deployment of the new on-line economic, political, and social era. Enabling the *Service Web* requires the development of techniques to address various challenging issues. Required techniques include services description, discovery, querying, composition, monitoring, security, and privacy [91]. This calls for a comprehensive *middleware* framework for managing *autonomous* and *heterogeneous* Web services. This process would be conducted *dynamically* and *transparently*. An epochal project that is currently under investigation at Virginia Tech concerns the architectural components of a *Web Service Management System* (*WSMS*). The overall aim of a *WSMS* is to provide for Web services what DBMSs have provided for data. Users no longer need to think in terms of *data* but rather *services*. Web services are treated as *first-class* objects that can be manipulated as if they were pieces of data. Our main focus in this book is to present a comprehensive query infrastructure for the efficient delivery of Web services. This query infrastructure constitutes a central component of the highly anticipated *WSMS*.

Web services may be tied to specific data sources or generic enough to operate with a wide range of data sources. They may also be part of legacy systems or newly developed systems that work with databases and other services. In fact, a large portion of information would be "hiding" behind Web services. Using Web services consists generally of invoking operations by sending and receiving messages. However, for complex applications accessing diverse Web services (e.g., a travel package), there is a need for an integrated and efficient way to manipulate and deliver Web services' functionalities. To address this challenge, we proposed a novel *query infrastructure* that offers complex query facilities over Web services [74, 73, 76]. In a nutshell, users submit *declarative* queries that are resolved through the combined invocations of different Web service operations. Queries target Web services and the information flow being exchanged during the invocation of their operations. The proposed query model would allow efficient integration across diverse Web services.

A first step in enabling such queries is to define a query model that facilitates the formulation and submission of queries and their transformation into actual invocations of Web service operations. We propose a three-level query model where users formulate queries through relations defined at the top level. Queries are then processed throughout the three levels until obtaining a *service execution plan* where Web services operations are invoked and their results combined.

In the proposed query infrastructure, the fundamental assumptions are that Web services are autonomous, highly volatile, *a priori* unknown, and their number is large. Autonomy means that Web services are independent and no particular behavior can be mandated on them. Web services are highly volatile as they are subject to frequent fluctuations during their lifetime (e.g., unavailability and changes in quality and performance.) More importantly, large numbers of Web services are expected to compete in offering "similar" functionalities under different conditions. A major challenge is then to devise the "*best*" combination of Web services with respect to the expected quality. Our *optimization model* is based on *Quality of Web Service (QoWS)* that would capture users' requirements for efficiency. The concept of quality of Web service (*QoWS*) is considered as a key feature in distinguishing between competing Web services [94]. *QoWS* encompasses different quality parameters that characterizes the behavior of a Web service in delivering its functionalities. Examples of parameters include availability, latency, and fees.

Several fluctuations may occur during a Web service lifetime. Thus, promised *QoWS* may not be always fulfilled. In general, small differences between delivered and advertised values may be acceptable for most users. However, large differences may be seen as a *performance* degradation for the Web service in delivering its functionalities. For that reason, we monitor *QoWS* for invoked Web services. This monitoring would essentially measure the fluctuations of *QoWS* parameters and give an assessment or rating for the Web service. Finally, for a given user request, we may not be able to find a Web service that offers an exact match. The approach proposes different levels of matching allowing a broader range of choices and flexibility in solving a query. This involves the use of ontologies to express the semantics of both requests and Web service offerings.

In the following, we outline major characteristics of the Web service environment that make building the proposed query infrastructure a challenging task.

- **Large service space** – Web services are proliferating at a very fast pace and are becoming ubiquitous for all kinds of human activities. Locating Web services of interest is hence an arduous task. Sifting through this large service space may not be feasible without an appropriate organization of Web services.
- **Autonomy and dynamism** – Web services are dynamic and independent entities. The query infrastructure cannot mandate any particular behavior on Web services to achieve its goal. No cooperation from Web services for optimization purposes may be assumed. In addition, adaptation to changes may be necessary while building and executing the service execution plan.
- **Web services competition** – Different categories of service providers will compete in offering similar functionalities. They will differ in terms of the Quality of Web Service (*QoWS*) under which they can deliver those functionalities. We need to provide the necessary mechanisms to select the best Web services and combinations of Web services.

Efficiently querying Web databases and Web services requires to tackle several challenging research issues. In the following, we outline those issues that we have addressed in our book (Figure 1.2).

- **Web databases space organization** – Due to the sheer size of the databases space, it is necessary to define an adequate organization that would foster efficiency in solving queries. This organization would filter interactions and allow to exploit the service space in a more tractable manner. It could be seen as a lightweight schema for the data space. Such organization should be easily deployable and support the inherent dynamism of the Web.

- **Web service based query model** – Users should be able to express their needs for service and information through simple queries. We need to devise a query model where Web services are treated as first class objects. This model defines the settings under which queries are formulated, submitted and finally resolved. The resolution process would lead to the invocation of actual Web services.

- **Optimization model** – Performance has a prime importance in successfully deploying a query infrastructure over Web services. We need to define an optimization model that would capture efficiency requirements in a Web services centric environment. Parameters and conditions that are relevant for defining "optimal" execution plans for queries will need to be devised. This will guide the conception of efficient techniques to achieve optimization. Recent literature [37, 83] shows that *Quality of Web Service* (QoWS) of individual Web services is crucial for their competitiveness. In addition, there is an increasing need to provide acceptable *Quality of Web Service* (QoWS) over Web applications. The concept of *QoWS* would capture more accurately users and applications' requirements for efficiency and hence for query optimization.

- **Web service monitoring** – Web services are highly volatile independent entities upon which users do not have any control. They may exhibit several fluctuations that may not be available from their description. This is especially true for their *QoWS*. This points to the need to monitor they behavior in terms of delivering the promised *QoWS*. This would be an important asset for the optimization model when making decisions on using specific Web services.

The major focus of our book is on supporting efficient querying and delivery of Web services on the Semantic Web. We also worked on Web databases querying at an early stage of our book. To achieve our goals, we looked at different issues and made several contributions. These contributions constitute the underlying infrastructure for a comprehensive query infrastructure for Web services. Although most of our examples are in the context of Digital Government, our solutions are generic enough to be applied in various domains including e-commerce with all its forms (B2B, B2C, etc.) In the following, we summarize the major contributions of our research (Figure 1.2).

- **Ontological organization of Web databases and Web services** – We propose a distributed ontology based organization for Web databases [72, 26]. This organization facilitates location and querying of Web databases. Web databases are organized and segmented based on simple ontologies that describe coherent slices of the information space. The main premise is that Web databases are built to serve specific purposes. Distributed ontologies of Web databases are established through a simple domain ontology. Inter-ontology relationships are dynamically established between ontologies. They can be viewed as a simplified way to share information with low overhead. In addition, intra-ontology relationships between Web databases are considered. This allows a more flexible and precise querying

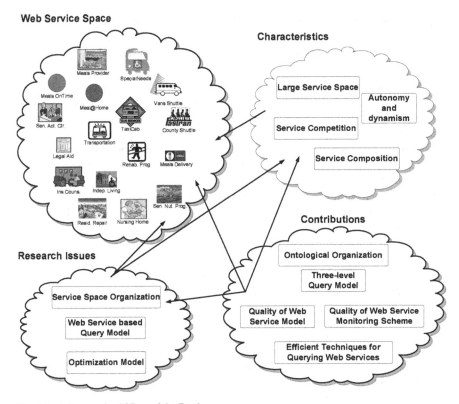

Fig. 1.2 A Summarized View of the Book

within an ontology. These relationships form a hierarchy of classes (an information type based classification hierarchy) inside an ontology.

- **Three-level query model for Web services** – We propose a query model adapted
  to Web services [74, 73, 76]. Users and applications would formulate declarative
  queries that are translated into invocations of different Web services operations.
  Also, based on some specific users' needs, it may not be always possible to find
  the exact Web service to fulfill that need. In addition, users may be willing to
  accept similar or close answers to their requests. Thus, instead of trying to only
  find an exact match for a query, we propose a more flexible matching scheme
  where some details of selected Web services differ from what is specified in the
  request.

- **Quality of Web service model** – Recent literature [94, 37, 83] shows that $QoWS$
  of individual Web services is crucial for their competitiveness. In addition, there
  is an increasing need to provide acceptable $QoWS$ over Web applications. The
  concept of $QoWS$ would capture more accurately users and applications' requirements for efficiency and hence for query optimization. The challenge is to define

appropriate metrics to characterize *QoWS* and devise techniques to measure that *QoS*. A comprehensive characterization of non-functional properties of Web services is proposed citeOB04a, OB03. This results in a model where Quality of Web Services are classified based on the Web service behavior they characterize.

- **Quality of Web service monitoring scheme** – *QoWS* may be subject to fluctuations during a Web service lifetime. Large differences may be seen as a performance degradation for the Web service in delivering its functionalities. We propose to monitor the *QoWS* of invoked Web services [74]. This monitoring would essentially measure the fluctuations of *QoWS* parameters and rate the Web services accordingly. Those ratings would be used during optimization to adjust the values of *QoWS* parameters.
- **Efficient techniques for querying Web services** – We propose different techniques to efficiently query Web services based on the quality of Web service model that we have defined [74, 73]. Several Web services may compete in offering similar functionalities. Since a query is solved by accessing different Web services, we need to take into account their quality of Web service and the eventual business partnerships that may exist between them. Business partnerships generally imply some privileges that may enhance the overall quality of the service execution plan (e.g., discounts).

To illustrate the need for a comprehensive query infrastructure over Web services, we consider the case of social services within the Virginia Department for the Aging[1]. We will also use examples from this scenario throughout the book. The Department for the Aging operates mainly through its Area Agencies of Aging (AAA) located in different counties and cities throughout the state. They are the first point of contact for senior citizens seeking support and social benefits. The scenario starts by illustrating how the different AAAs are currently functioning and highlight the many challenges facing self-sufficiency workers and senior citizens alike. We then outline how our approach for efficient delivery of Web services would help to achieve the maximum efficiency for the AAAs and the best services for senior citizens.

Let us assume that Maria, an indigent senior citizen, would like to receive services from the Department for the Aging. She would have to visit the local AAA at Mountain county for an interview (Figure 1.3). There, Peter a self-sufficiency worker would conduct the interview by asking for a list of documents and information from Maria. Based on his expertise and using different means (manuals, online databases, etc.), Peter evaluates Maria's needs. He finds out that Maria is potentially qualified for the following benefits, most of which are sub-contracted from outside organizations (mostly non-profit organizations and businesses but also other government agencies): *transportation for the elderly and handicapped, meals provider, meals delivery, senior activity center, residential repair, nursing home, senior nutrition program, insurance counseling,* and *legal aid.*

---

[1] This was part of a project between Virginia Tech and the Virginia Department for the Aging in the State of Virginia.

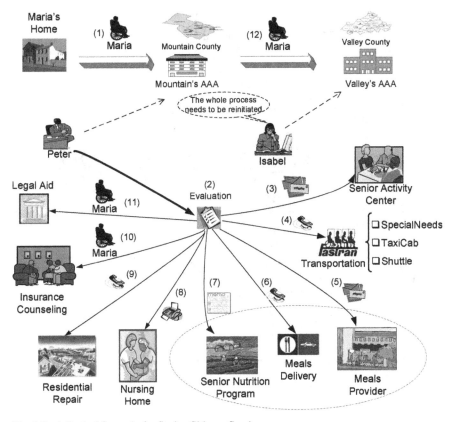

Fig. 1.3 A Typical Scenario for Senior Citizens Services

After the eligibility check, Peter has to select an appropriate provider for each service. Several potential providers may be candidates. He then needs to contact those selected providers individually to check if they meet the AAA's requirements (e.g., budget) and are actually able to serve Maria's needs. Communication with providers takes place using various media including snail mail, email, fax, and phone. The choice of the provider is mostly based on Peter's expertise and some information gathered through different means (e.g., Web sites, brochures). This may not be an easy task for the self-sufficiency worker. For example, the *transportation* service may be provided by different transportation companies (Figure 1.4): County Shuttle – a county service that provides free rides for senior citizens and other eligible persons but has limited coverage, Vans Shuttle – a private shuttle company that charges a monthly fee, TaxiCab – offers flat fee for any use of a taxi cab, SpecialNeeds – a specialized transportation company for the handicapped. Although all these providers offer transportation services, the conditions (e.g., price,

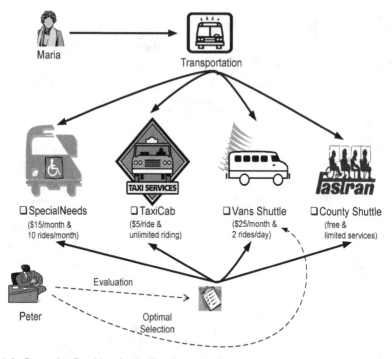

Fig. 1.4 Competing Providers for the Transportation Service

quality) under which those services are offered may differ. For instance, the Vans Shuttle company may be the least expensive but may not provide the same level of service for handicapped persons as the specialized company.

This difficult process of looking for the best providers can be further exacerbating if Maria's situation changes. For example, assume that Maria gets involved in a car accident and becomes wheelchair confined (Figure 1.5). In this case, the self-sufficiency worker has to adapt the different services to Maria's new situation. This means, for instance, that the provider for transportation service may need to be changed. In this case, SpecialNeeds is selected instead of Vans Shuttle. In addition, Peter finds out that Maria may be eligible for new services: *Independent Living* – a service to maximize the integration of disabled citizens in community leadership, independence, and productivity, and *Rehabilitation Program* – a therapy program for physical and emotional rehabilitation of disabled citizens. Again, Peter would need to select the best providers and contact them individually to check if they effectively meet AAA's requirements and Maria's needs. Another major change occurs if Maria decides to move to another county, namely Valley county (Figure 1.3). Once there, she needs to visit the local AAA again. The self-sufficiency worker at Valley's AAA, Isabel, would have to (re)initiate the whole process from scratch.

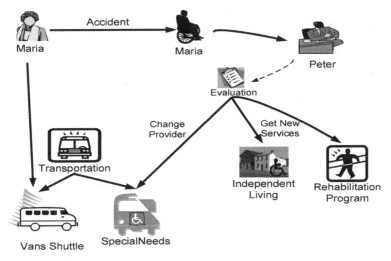

Fig. 1.5 Consumer Context Changes

Caring for the nutritional needs (Figure 1.6) of Maria may require three types of services *Meals Provider*, *Meals Delivery*, and *Senior Nutrition Program*. In this case, individual providers for each type will be selected in a way that optimizes their combination. For instance, the choice of Meal@Home as a *meals provider* may reduce costs if combined with MealsOnTime as the *meals delivery* provider. These two providers are in business partnership to provide discounts for their common customers.

In summary, for any particular service that Maria is qualified for, either at Mountain or Valley counties, several potential providers may exist. Although they may offer similar services, the conditions (e.g., price, quality) under which those services are offered may differ. Manually looking for the appropriate providers (either individually or in combination) is an error-prone process that may lead to sub-optimal outcomes for both the agency and the senior citizens. This is especially critical as AAAs work generally with tight funding. In addition, as Maria's situation changes, it might be necessary to modify existing services and add new ones. Furthermore, as provider quality changes over time and new providers are available or become unavailable, the AAA may decide to change Maria's providers for cost purposes.

Governments already outsource most of their functions to the private sector (businesses and non-profit institutions) to achieve maximum cost efficiency. A comprehensive framework to automatically and dynamically deliver the best Web services is still lacking. This is especially needed as several providers would compete for this burgeoning market. We propose to build a system that continuously searches for the best services at any given point in time. Providers would channel their offerings through Web services. Web services are deemed to be the choice by excellence for government agencies and businesses to conduct all forms of interactions on the

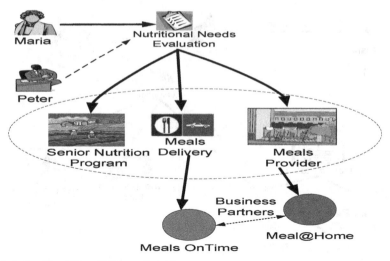

Fig. 1.6 Combined Use of Different Providers

Web. In essence, there is a need for a system that would allow to tap easily and uniformly into the continuously growing Web services space by treating Web services as *first class objects*. A central issue is to select the best Web services and combine them in an optimal way. This especially entails *efficient querying* of Web services. The self-sufficiency worker and even the senior citizen would only have to express their needs through simple, yet powerful, declarative queries over a well defined interface. Our ultimate goal is to develop a generic approach for optimally querying Web services.

Organization of the Book

In Chapter 2, we propose a distributed ontology based organization of Web databases. The distributed ontology caters for the meaningful organization of and efficient access to Web databases. In our approach, each database has a *co-database* attached to it. A co-database (meta–information repository) is an XML-enabled database that stores information about its associated database, ontologies and inter-ontology relationships of that database. The proposed distributed ontology has been fully implemented in WebFINDIT. We present the salient features of the WebFINDIT system and its deployment over a large number of database systems.

In Chapter 3, we propose a novel query model for Web services. The main idea of this model is the abstraction of the *Service Space* into three levels, namely *query*, *virtual*, and *concrete*. This would represent a sort of schema for the service space. We then propose a multi-mode matching process to allow close and partial answers.

In Chapter 4, we present a holistic approach for the problem of query optimization for Web services. We consider several non functional properties in selecting and combining Web services. These are *Quality of Web Service* parameters. We use a monitoring technique to assess the behavior of Web services in delivering their functionalities and abiding to their promised *QoWS*. We then present several algorithms for optimizing Web service queries based on *QoWS*.

In Chapter 5, we describe the implementation of our approach for efficiently querying Web services in WebDG system. We also present an analytical study for the different algorithms presented in Chapter 5. Finally, we conduct extensive experiments for these algorithms to asses their performance and compare their results.

In Chapter 6, we present a survey on several research areas related to this book including Web databases integration and efficient querying, as well as Web service querying, composition, and optimization.

In Chapter 7, we conclude our book and present some promising future research.

Chapter 2
Ontological Organization of Web Databases

Organizations rely on a wide variety of databases to conduct their everyday business. Databases are usually designed from scratch if none is found to meet requirements. This has led to a proliferation of databases obeying different sets of requirements oftentimes modeling the same situations. In many instances, and because of a lack of any *organized* conglomeration of databases, users create their own pieces of information that may exist in current databases. Though it may be known where a certain piece of information is stored, locating it may be prohibitive. Sharing information across heterogeneous platforms is not an issue anymore due to the readily available and relatively cheap network connectivity. Although one may *potentially* access all participating databases, in reality this is an almost intractable task due to various fundamental problems [28, 22]. The challenge is to give users the sense that they are accessing a single database that contains almost everything he or she needs.

The Internet has solved the age-old problem of network connectivity and thus enabling the potential access to, and data sharing among large numbers of databases. However, enabling users to discover useful information requires an adequate *metadata* infrastructure that must scale with the diversity and dynamism of both users' interests and Internet accessible databases. To allow effective and efficient data sharing on the Web, we need an infrastructure that can support flexible tools for information space organization, communication facilities, information discovery, content description, and assembly of data from heterogeneous sources. Previous techniques for manipulating these sources are not appropriate and efficient. Users needs tools for the logical and scalable exploration of such systems in a three step process involving: (i) *Location* of appropriate information sources; (ii) *Searching* of these sources for relevant information items; (iii) *Understanding* of the structure, terminology and patterns of use of these information items for data integration, and ultimately, querying.

In our approach, ontologies of information repositories are established through a simple domain ontology [72]. This meta–information represents the domain of interest of the underlying information repositories. For example, collection of databases that store information about the same topic are grouped together. Individual databases join and leave the formed ontologies at their own discretion. The proposed ontological organization constitutes the foundation of the WebFINDIT prototype [24, 26, 25]. WebFINDIT provides a scalable and portable architecture using the latest in distributed object and Web technologies, including CORBA as a distributed computing platform, Java, and connectivity gateways to access native information sources.

In this chapter, we present a model that partitions the information space into a distributed, highly specialized domain ontologies. We also introduce inter-ontology relationships to cater for user-based interests across ontologies defined over Internet databases. We also describe an architecture that implements these two fundamental constructs over Internet databases. The aim of the proposed model and architecture is to eventually facilitate data discovery and sharing for Internet databases.

2.1 Information Space Organization and Modeling

Organizing Web databases into distributed ontologies is mainly motivated by the fact that in a highly dynamic and constantly growing network of databases accessible through the Web, there is a need for a meaningful organization and segmentation of the information space. We adopt an ontology-based organization of the diverse databases to filter interactions, accelerate information searches, and allow for the sharing of data in a tractable manner [72]. Key criteria that have guided our approach are: scalability, design simplicity, and easy to use structuring mechanisms based on object-orientation.

The information space is organized through distributed domain ontologies. Databases join and leave a given ontology based on their domains of interest which represent some portion of the information space. For example, databases that share the topic Medical Research are linked to the same ontology. This topic-based ontology provides the terminology for formulating queries involving a specific area of interest. Such organization aims to reduce the overhead of locating and querying information in large networks of databases. As a database may contain information related to more than one domain of interest, it may be linked to more than one ontology at the same time.

The different ontology formed on the above principle are not isolated entities but they can be related to each other by inter-ontology relationships. These relationships are created based on the users' needs. They allow a user query to be resolved by databases in remote ontologies when it cannot be resolved locally.

We do not intend to achieve an automatic "reconciliation" between heterogeneous ontologies. In our system, users incrementally learn about the available information space by browsing the local ontology and by following the inter-ontology relationships. In this way, they have sufficient information to query actual data.

2.1.1 Domain Models

Each ontology is specialized into a single common area of interest. It provides domain specific information and terms for interacting within the ontology and its underlying databases. That is providing an abstraction of a specific domain. This abstraction is intended to be used by users and other ontologies as a description of the specific domain. Ontologies dynamically clump databases together based on common areas of interest into a single atomic unit. This generates a *conceptual space* which has a specific content and scope. The formation, dissolution and modification of an ontology is a semi-automatic process. Privileged users (e.g., the database administrators) are provided with tools to maintain the different ontologies mainly on a negotiation basis.

Instead of considering a simple membership of databases to an ontology, intra-ontology relationships between these sources are considered. This allows a more flexible and precise querying within an ontology. These relationships form a hierarchy of classes (an information type based classification hierarchy) inside an ontology. In that respect, users can refine their queries by browsing the different classes of an ontology.

2.1.2 Inter-ontology Relationships

When a user submits a query to the local ontology, it might be not resolvable locally. In this case, the system try to find remote ontologies that can eventually resolve the query. In order to allow such query "migration", inter-ontology relationships are dynamically established between two ontologies based on users' needs. Inter-ontology relationships can be viewed as a simplified way to share information with low overhead. The amount of sharing in an inter-ontology relationship will typically involve a minimum amount of information exchange.

Although the above relationships involve basically only ontologies, they are extended to databases as well. This allows more flexibility in the organization and querying of the information space. Inter-ontology relationships are of three types (see Figure 2.1). The first type involves a relationship between two ontologies to exchange information. The second type involves a relationship between two databases. The third type involves a relationship between an ontology and a database. An inter-ontology relationship between two ontologies involves providing a general description of the information that is to be shared. Likewise, an inter-ontology relationship between two databases also involves providing a general description of information that databases would like to share. The third alternative is a relationship between an ontology and a database. In this case, the database (or the ontology) provides a general description of the information it is willing to share with the ontology (or database). The difference between these three alternatives lies in the way queries are resolved. In the first and third alternative (when the information provider is an ontology), the providing ontology takes over to further resolve the query. In the second case, however, the user is responsible for contacting the providing database in order to gain knowledge about the information.

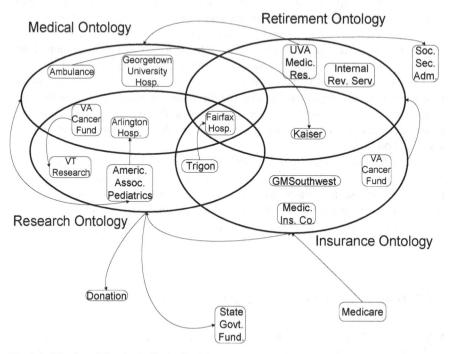

Fig. 2.1 Distributed Ontologies in the Healthcare Domain

Our dynamic distributed ontologies make information accessing more tractable by limiting the number of databases which must interact. Databases join and leave ontologies and inter-ontology relationships based upon local requirements and constraints. At any given point in time a single database may partake in several ontologies and inter-ontology relationships.

We believe that a complete reconciliation between all the databases accessible through the Web is not a tractable problem. In our approach, there is no automatic translation between different ontologies. Users are incrementally educated about the available information space. They discover and become familiar with the databases that are effectively relevant. They can submit precise queries which guarantee that only relevant answers are returned. On the other hand, databases join simply our distributed ontologies by providing some local information and choosing one or more ontologies that meet their interests. In addition, this join does not involve major modifications in the overall system – we only need to made some changes at the metadata level related to the involved ontologies. This allows our system to scale easily and to be queried in a simple and flexible way.

2.1.3 Information Sources Modeling

When a database decides to join the distributed ontologies, it has to define which areas are of interest for it. Links are then established to ontologies implementing these concepts if any, otherwise a negotiation may be engaged with other databases to form new ontologies. The database administrator must provide an object-oriented view of the underlying database. This view contains the terms of interest available from that database. These terms provide the interface that can be used to communicate with the database. More specifically, this view consists of one or several types (called access interface of a database) containing the exported operations (attributes and functions) and a textual description of these operations. The membership of a database to an ontology is materialized by the fact that the database is an instance of one or many classes in the same or different ontologies. We should also note that other useful information are provided by the database administrator (see Section 2.3).

To illustrate the way a database is modeled and is related to the domain model, consider the `Virginia Cancer Fund` database which is member of the ontology `Research` (see Figure 2.1). Let us assume that this database is an instance of a class in the ontology `Research`. It represents, for example, an mSQL database that contains the following relations:

CancerClassify (`Cancer Id, Scientific Name, Common Name, Infection Area, Cause Known, Hereditary, Description`)
ResearchGroup (`Group Id, Cancer Id, Start Date, Supervisor Id`)
Staff (`Staff Id, Title, Name, Location, Phone, Research Field`)
GroupOwnership (`Ownership Id, Group Id, Staff Id, Date Commenced, Date Completed`)
Funding (`Funding Id, Group Id, Provider Name, Amount, Conditions`)
ResearchResults (`Result Id, Group Id, Results Date, Description`)

If the database administrator decides to make public some information related to some of the above relations, they have to be advertised by specifying the information type to be published as follows:

```
Type Funding {
    attribute string CancerClassify.CommonName;
    function real Amount(string
                         CancerClassify.CommonName);
}

Type Results {
```

```
       attribute string Staff.Name;
       attribute int GroupOwnership.DateCommenced;
       function string  Description(string Staff.Name,
                        intDate
                        GroupOwnership.Datecommenced);
   }
```

Note that the textual explanations of the attributes and operations are left out of the description for clarity. Each attribute denotes a relation field and each function denotes an access routine to the database. The implementation of these features is transparent to the user. For instance, the function `Description()` denotes the access routine that returns the description of all results obtained by a staff member after a given date. This routine is written in mSQL's C interface. In the case of an object-oriented database, an attribute denotes a class attribute and a function denotes either a class method or an access routine. Thus, users can locate the database, then investigate its exported interface and fetch useful attributes and functions to access the database.

2.2 Inter-Ontology Relationships Maintenance

2.2.1 Dynamically Linking Databases and Ontologies

It is important that WebFINDIT allow for an adaptive evolution of the organization of the inherently dynamic information space. The adaptive evolution is necessary to provide support for discovery of meta-meta data, meta- data, and data. To maintain and update the dynamic relationships between ontologies and/or databases, WebFINDIT uses distributed agents. They act independently of other system components [33]. They monitor the system and user behavior and formulate a strategy for the creation or removal of inter-ontology relationships. It is assumed that the agents are always running. For instance, among agents' tasks is to determine whether a new inter-ontology relationship is needed. This is achieved by monitoring the traffic over inter-ontology relationships and checking whether the destination is final based on users' activity. On the one hand, if an inter-ontology relationship is rarely used, then it is most likely to be stale. The agent would recommend its removal. In what follows, we elaborate on the processes of creating and deleting inter-ontology relationships.

2.2.2 Creating inter-ontology relationships

Figure 2.2 illustrates a scenario where a new inter-ontology relationship is created. In this scenario, the ontology Mental Illness and Addiction has an outgoing inter-ontology relationship with Medicaid, which in turn has an outgoing inter-ontology relationship with Low Income. During the execution of the system, the monitoring agents discover the following: The majority of users who begin their query session from Mental Illness and Addiction and traverse the inter-ontology relationship between Mental Illness and Addiction and Medicaid do not initiate queries on the ontology Medicaid. Rather, they use the inter-ontology relationship between Medicaid and Low Income to go to the Low Income ontology, where they do initiate queries. In this case, observing that the ontology Medicaid is being used as a bridge between Mental Illness and Addiction and Low Income, the monitoring agents would recommend the creation of a new inter-ontology relationship from Mental Illness and Addiction to Low Income. This would allow users to navigate directly from Mental Illness and Addiction to Low Income and reduce the number of traversed nodes to reach relevant ontologies.

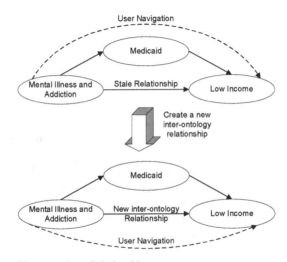

Fig. 2.2 Creation of Inter-ontology Relationships

2.2.3 Deleting inter-ontology relationships

If an inter-ontology relationship is rarely used or always leads to a non-relevant ontology, then it is considered to be a stale relationship. In this case, a monitoring agent would recommend the deletion of the inter-ontology relationship. Consider the example of Figure 2.3. The ontology At Risk Children has an outgoing inter-ontology relationship with the ontology Low Income, which in turn has an outgoing inter-ontology relationship with the ontology Local Health and Human Services. Monitoring agents of these ontologies report the following: The majority of users who

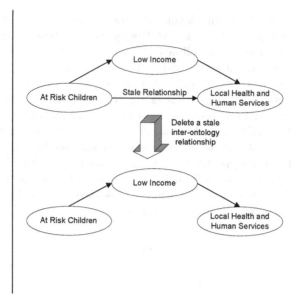

Fig. 2.3 Deletion of Inter-ontology Relationships

navigate directly from At Risk Children to Local Health and Human Services ultimately leave Local Health and Human Services without performing any query. This
suggests that the direct link between At Risk Children and Local Health and Human
Services is not a useful link. The agents would therefore recommend the deletion of
the inter-ontology relationship between At Risk Children and Local Health and Human Services. Local Health and Human Services would still be navigable from At
Risk Children via Low Income, but the overhead associated with a stale link would
have been eliminated.

2.3 Providing Metadata Support through the Concept of
Co-Databases

Co–databases are introduced as a means for implementing our distributed ontology
concept and as an aid to inter–site data sharing. These are metadata repositories that
surround each local DBMS, and which know a system's capability and functionality. Formation of information space relationships (i.e, ontologies and inter-ontology
relationships) and maintenance as well as exploration of these relationships occur
via a special-purpose language called *WebTassili*. An overview of the WebTassili
language is presented in Section 2.4.

Locating a set of databases that fit user queries requires detailed information about the content of each database in the system. To avoid the problem of

centralized administration of information, meta–information repositories are distributed over information networks. In our approach, each participating database has a *co-database* attached to it. A co-database (meta–information repository) is an XML-enabled database that stores information about its associated database, ontologies and inter-ontology relationships of this database. A set of databases exporting a certain type of information is represented by a class in the co-database schema. This also means that an ontology is represented by a class or a hierarchy of classes (i.e., information type based on a classification hierarchy).

A typical co-database schema contains subschemas that represent ontologies and inter-ontology relationships that deal with specific types of information (see Figure 2.4). The first sub-schema consists of a tree of classes where each class represents a set of databases that can answer queries about a specialized type of information. This subschema represents ontologies. The class `Ontologies Root` forms the root of the ontologies tree. Every subclass of the class `Ontologies` represents the root of an ontology tree. Every node in that tree represents a specific information type. An ontology is hierarchically organized in the form of a tree, so that an information type has a number of subordinate information types and at most one superior information type. This organization allows an ontology to be structured according to a specialization relationship. For instance, the class `Research` could have two subclasses `Cancer Research` and `Child Research`. The classes joined in the ontology tree support each other in answering queries directed to them. If a user query conforms better with the information type of a given subclass, then the query will be forwarded to this subclass. If no classes are found in the ontology tree while handling a user query, then either the user simplifies the query or the query is forwarded to other ontologies (or databases) via inter–ontology relationships. The splitting of an ontology into smaller units increases the efficiency when searching information types.

The co-database also contains another type of subschema. This subschema consists on the one hand, of a subschema of inter-ontology relationships that involve the ontology the database is member of; and on the other hand of a subschema of inter-ontology relationships that involve the database itself. Each of these subschemas consists in turn of two subclasses that respectively describe inter-ontology relationships with databases and inter-ontology relationships with other ontologies.

In particular, every class in an ontology tree contains a description about the participating databases and the type of information they contain. Description of the databases will include information about the data model, operating system, query language, etc. Description of the information type will include its general structure and behavior. We should also mention that the documentation (demo) associated with each information instance is stored in actual databases. This is done for two reasons: (1) Database autonomy is maintained and, (2) documentations can be modified with little or no overhead on the associated co-databases.

The class `Ontology Root` contains the generic attributes that are inherited by all classes in the ontology tree. A subset of the attributes of the class `Ontology Root` is:

Class Ontology Root {

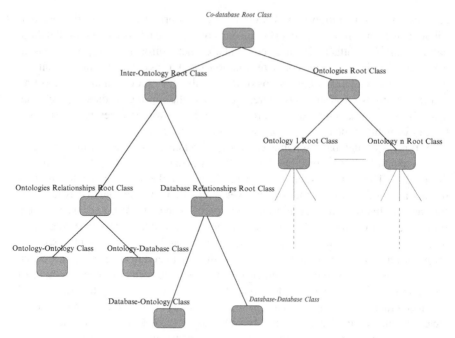

Fig. 2.4 The Outline of a Typical Co-Database Schema

      attribute string Information-type;
      attribute set(string) Synonyms;
      attribute string DBMS;
      attribute string Operating-system;
      attribute string Query-language;
      attribute set(string) Sub-information-types;
      attribute set(Inter-ontology Root)
               Inter-ontology Relationships;
      attribute set(Ontology Root) Members;
      ....
  }

The attribute Information-type represents the name of the information-type (e.g., ''Research'' for all instances of the class Research). The attribute Synonyms describes the set of alternative descriptions of each information-type. Users can use these descriptions to the effect of obtaining databases that provide information about the associated information type. The attribute Sub-information-types describes specialization relationship. The other attributes are self-explained.

Every sub-class of the class Ontology Root has some specific attributes that describe the domain model of the related set of underlying databases. These attributes do not necessarily correspond directly to the objects described in any particular database. For example, a subset of the attributes of the class `Research` (`Project` and `Grant` are two types defined elsewhere) is:

> **Class** `Research` **Isa** `Ontology Root{`
>   **attribute** `string Subject;`
>   **attribute** `set(Project) Projects;`
>   **attribute** `set(Grant) Funding;`
>   `.........`
> `}`

In Figure 2.4, the class `Inter-Ontology Root` contains the generic attributes that are relevant to all types of inter-ontology relationships. These relationships can be used to answer queries when the local ontology cannot answer them. An inter-ontology relationship can be seen as an intersection (or overlap) relationship between the related entities. Synonyms and generalization/specialization can be seen as intra-ontology relationships compared to the inter-ontology relationships. A subset of attributes of the class `Inter-Ontology Root` is:

> **Class** `Inter-Ontology Root {`
>   **attribute** `set(string) Description;`
>   **attribute** `string Point-of-entry;`
>   **attribute** `string Source;`
>   **attribute** `string Target;`
>   `.........`
> `}`

The attribute `Description` contains the information type that can be provided using the inter-ontology relationship. Assume that the user queries the ontology `Medical` about `Medical Insurance`. The use of the synonyms and generalization/specialization relationships fails to answer the user query. However, the ontology `Medical` has an inter–ontology relationship with the ontology `Insurance` where the value of the attribute `Description` is {``Health Insurance'', ``Medical Insurance''}. It is clear that this inter-ontology relationship provides the answer to the user query. The attribute `Point-of-entry` represents the name of the co-database that must be contacted to answer the query. The attribute `Source` and `Target` are self-explained.

So far, we presented the metadata model used to describe the ontologies and their relationships. In what follows, we will present how a particular database is described and linked to its ontologies. For example, the co-database attached to the `Fairfax Hospital` database contains information about all related ontologies and inter-ontology relationships. As the `Fairfax Hospital` database is member of two ontologies `Research` and `Medical`, it stores information about these two ontologies. This co-database contains also information about other ontologies and databases that have a relationship with these two ontologies and the database itself. The co-database stores information about the inter-ontology relationships `State Government Funding` database and `Insurance` ontology. It stores also access information of the `Fairfax Hospital` database, which includes the exported interface and the Internet address. The interface of a database consists of a set of types containing the exported operations and a textual description of these types. The database will be advertised through the co-database by specifying the information type, the documentation (a file containing multimedia data or a program that plays a product demonstration), and the access information which includes its location, the wrapper (a program allowing access to data in the database), and the set of exported types.

> **Information Source** `Fairfax Hospital` {
>   **Information Type** `'Research and Medical'`
>   **Documentation** `'http://www.nvc.cs.vt.edu/Fairfax'`
>   **Location** `'pluto.nvc.cs.vt.edu'`
>   **Wrapper** `'pluto.nvc.cs.vt.edu/WebTassiliOracle'`
>   **Interface** `ResearchProjects, PatientHistory`
>   }

The URL `''http://www.nvc.cs.vt.edu/Fairfax''` contains the documentation about `Fairfax Hospital` database. It contains any type of presentation accessible through the Web (e.g., a Java applet that plays a video clip). WebTassiliOracle is the wrapper needed to access data in the Oracle database using a WebTassili query. The exported interface contains two types that will be advertised as explained in the previous section for the `Virginia Cancer Fund` database.

The interface of a database can be used to query data stored in this database. This is possible only after locating this database as a relevant database. As pointed out before each sub-class of the class `Ontology Root` has a set of attributes that describe the domain model of the underlying databases. In fact, these attributes can also be used to query data stored in the underlying databases. However, these attributes do not correspond directly to attributes in database interfaces. For this reason, we define the relationships between database types and ontology domain model attributes. We call these relationships *mappings*. More specifically, there exists one mapping for each type in the interface of a database. These mappings are used to translate an ontology query into a set of queries to the relevant databases. Note that an attribute (or a function) in the type of a database may be related to different attributes (or functions) in different ontologies. For example, the attribute `Patient.name` of the type `PatientHistory` may be related to two domain attributes, one (a1) in the ontology `Medical` and another (a2) in the ontology `Research`. This can be described as follows:

> **Mapping** `PatientHistory` {
>   **attribute** `string Patient.Name` **Is** $<$ `Research.a1,`
>   `Medical.a2>;`
>   }

Information sharing is achieved through co-databases communicating with each other. As mentioned above, a database may belong to more than one ontology. In this case, its co-database will contain information about all ontologies it belongs to. Two databases can belong to the same ontology and still have different co-databases. This is true because these databases might belong to different ontologies and be involved with different inter-ontology relationships. This is one reason it is desirable that each database has one co-database attached to it instead of having one single co-database for each ontology. Database autonomy and high information availability are other reasons why it is not desirable to physically centralize the co-database.

2.4 Language Support for Distributed Ontologies of Web Databases

SQL and extensions thereof work best when the database schemas are known to the user. In that respect, it is not concerned with *discovering* metadata. Querying with SQL is done in one *single* step to get the data. In contrast, access to Web databases will happen in *two* steps and *iteratively*. In addition, the nature of the ontology architecture calls for a special handling of ontology and inter-ontology relationships management. To our knowledge, no language has been developed to support the access and management of ontologies in the context of Web databases. In what follows, we briefly introduce the main features of the WebTassili language. We focus on aspects designed specifically on helping users learn about the information sources content and location in distributed ontologies. Details about the language is outside the scope of this book.

WebTassili has been designed to address issues related to the use, design and evolution of WebFINDIT. The world of users is partitioned into privileged users and general users. Queries are resolved through an interactive process. Privileged users, such as administrators, can issue both data definition and data manipulation operations. The formation of ontologies and inter-ontology relationships, as well as co-database schema evolution, is achieved through the *WebTassili* data definition operations. An ontology is bootstrapped after formal negotiation between privileged users takes place. The ontology/inter-ontology schema is stored and maintained in individual co-databases. As co-databases contains replicated data, schema updates are then propagated to the appropriate co-databases using a predefined set of protocols. This data is then accessed by the component information repository to provide users with information regarding the structure of the system and the nature of databases. General users may issue read-only queries. The distributed updating and querying of co-databases is achieved via an interface process which allows interactions with remote sites.

WebTassili consists of both data definition and manipulation constructs. As for data definition features, it is used to define the different schemas and their intrinsic relationships. It provides constructs to define classes of information types and their corresponding relationships. In conventional object-oriented databases, the behavior of a class is the same for all its instances. WebTassili also provides mechanisms for defining constraints and firing triggers for evolution purposes. This feature is used to evolve schemas as well as propagate changes to related schemas. Data definition queries are only accessible to a selected number of users (administrators). The formation of a schema is achieved through a negotiation process. In that respect, WebTassili provides features for administrators to form and evolve schemas. More specifically, WebTassili provides the following data definition operations:

- Define classes and objects (structure and behavior).
- Define operations for schema evolution.
- Define operations for negotiation for schema creation and instantiation.

WebTassili is also used to manipulate the schema states. Users use WebTassili to query the structure and behavior of meta–information types. Users also use this query language to query information about participating databases. The manipulation in WebTassili is on both meta data and actual data. More specifically, WebTassili provides the following manipulation operations:

- Search for an information type.
- Search for an information type while providing its structure.
- Search for an information type while providing its structure and/or information about the host databases.
- Query remote databases

2.4.1 Information Discovery

We consider an example from the distributed ontologies that represent the medical information domain represented in Figure 2.1. Assume that physicians in the Fairfax Hospital are interested in gathering some information about the cancer disease in Virginia (Research, treatment, costs, insurance, etc.) For that purpose, they will use WebFINDIT in order to gather needed information. They will go through an interactive process using the WebTassili language.

Suppose now that one of the physicians at Fairfax Hospital queries WebFINDIT for medical research related to cancer disease. For this purpose, he or she can starts his or her investigation by submitting the following WebTassili query:

Find Ontologies With Information Medical Research;

In order to resolve this query, WebFINDIT starts from the ontologies the Fairfax Hospital is member of and checks if they hold the information. The system found that one of the local ontologies, the Research ontology, deals with this type of information. Refinement (if needed) is performed until the specific information type is found. As the user is interested in more specific information i.e., medical research on cancer, he or she submit a refinement query (find more specific information type) as follows:

Display SubClasses of Class Medical Research;

The ontology or class `Medical Research` shows that it contains the sub-classes: `Cancer Research`, `Child Research` and `AIDS Research`. The user can then decide to query one of the displayed classes or continue the refinement process. As the user is interested in the first subclass, she or he issues the following query to display instances of this subclass:

Display Instance of Class `Cancer Research`;

The user is then faced with too many instances of the subclass `Cancer Research` contained in many databases. Assume that she or he decides to query the `Arlington Hospital` database which is a instance of that subclass. Before that, the user can become more knowledgeable about this database using a WebTassili construct that displays the documentation of this information. WebTassili provides a construct for displaying the documentation of this information. An example of this query is:

Display Document of Instance `Arlington Hospital`
Of Class `Cancer Research`;

Assuming the user finds a database that contains the requested information, attributes and functions are provided to directly access the database for an instance of this information type. WebTassili provides users with primitives to manipulate data drawn from diverse databases. Users use local functions to directly access the providing databases to get the actual data. In our example, if the user is interested in querying the database `Virginia Cancer Fund` from the class `Cancer Research` of the ontology `Research`, he or she uses the following WebTassili query to display the interface exported by the database:

Display Access Information of Instance `Virginia Cancer Fund`
Of Class `Cancer Research`;

At this point, the user is completely aware of this database. She or he knows the location of this database and how to access it to get actual data and some other useful information. The database `Virginia Cancer Fund` is located at `''mars.nvc.cs.vt.edu''` and exports several types. Below is as an example of an exported type:

```
Type Funding {
    attribute string CancerClassify.CommonName;
    function real Amount(string
                         CancerClassify.CommonName);
}
```

The function `Amount()` returns the total budget of a given research project. For instance, if we are interested in the budget of the research project `Lung Cancer`, we use the function `Amount(''Lung Cancer'')`. This function is translated to the following SQL query (the native query language of the underlying database):

```
Select c.Amount
From CancerClassify a, ResearchGroup b, Funding c
Where a.CommonName = ''Lung Cancer''
and    a.CancerId = b.CancerId
and    b.GroupId = c.GroupId
```

In the above scenario, the user was involved in a browsing session to discover the databases of interest inside the ontology `Research`. If this ontology contains a large number of databases, then browsing the description (documentation or access information) of the underlying databases may be unrealistic. In such a case, the user may be interested to query the data stored in these databases using the domain attributes of the ontology. For example, to the effect of obtaining the name of projects related to `Cancer`, the user can type the following WebTassili query:

```
Select r.Projects.name
Ontologies Research r
Where r.Subject = ''Cancer''
```

This query is expressed using the domain model of the ontology `Research`. The system uses the mappings (as defined in Section 2.3) to translate this query into a set of queries to the relevant databases that are members of the ontology.

Assume now that another physician is interested in querying the system about private medical insurance. The following query is submitted to the system.

Find Ontologies With Information `Insurance`;

As usually, WebFINDIT first checks the ontologies the `Fairfax Hospital` is member of. The two local ontologies `Research` and `Medical` fail to answer the query. WebFINDIT finds that there is an inter-ontology relationship with another ontology `Insurance` that appears to deal with the requested information type. A point of entry is provided for this ontology. In this way, an inter-ontology relationship contains the resources that are available to an ontology to answer requests when they cannot be handled locally. To establish a connection with a remote ontology, a user uses the following WebTassili query:

Connect To Ontology `Insurance`;

The user is now able to investigate this ontology looking for more relevant information. After some refinements, a database is selected and queried as in the first part of the example.

2.4.2 Ontology Interaction and Negotiation

Ontologies and inter-ontology relationships provide the means for dynamically synchronizing database interactions in a decentralized manner. By joining an ontology, databases implicitly *agree* to work together. Databases retain control, and join or leave ontologies/inter-ontology relationships based upon local considerations. The forming, joining, and leaving of ontologies and inter-ontology relationships is controlled by privileged users (database administrators).

In some instances, users may ask about information that is not in the local domain of interest. If these requests are small, a mapping between a set of information meta types to an ontology via an inter-ontology relationships is enough to resolve the query. If the number of requests remains high the database administrator may, for efficiency reasons, investigate the formation of an ontology with the "popular" remote databases or join a pre-existing ontology. Alternatively, the database administrator may initiate a negotiation with other database members to establish an inter-ontology relationship with an existing ontology or database.

Assume that the GMSouthwest database of the ontology Insurance wants to establish an inter-ontology relationship with the ontology Medical. To initiate a negotiation with this ontology, the following WebTassili query is used:

Inquire at Ontology Medical;

To send the requested information (i.e., remote structural information) to the servicing Medical, the representative (administrator site) database uses the following query:

Send to GMSouthwest
Object Medical.template;

The negotiation process ends (establishment of an inter-ontology relationship or not) whenever the involved entities decide so. Other primitives exist to remove methods and objects when a database relinquishes access to local information. There are also more basic primitives which are used to establish an ontology and propagate and validate changes. Each operation must be validated by all participating administrators. The instantiation operation is an exception. In this case the database described by an object is the one that decides what the object state should be. If there is disagreement in the validation process, the administrator who instigated the operation will choose the course of action to be taken.

A joining database must provide some information about the data it would like to share, as well as information about itself. If the new information repository is accepted as a member, the administrator of the ontology will then decide how the ontology schema is to be changed. During this informal exchange, many parameters need to be set. For instance, a threshold for the minimum and maximum number of ontology members is negotiated and set. Likewise, a threshold on the minimum and maximum number of inter-ontology relationships with information sources and ontologies is also set.

Initially, an administrator is selected to create the root class of the ontology schema. Once this is done, the root of the schema is sent to every participating information repository for validation. Based on feedback from the group, the creator will decide whether to change the object or not. This process will continue until there is a consensus. Changes are only made at a single site until consensus is achieved - at which time the change is made persistent and propagated to the appropriate databases. If existing classes/methods are to be updated, responsibility lies with the information repository that "owns" it.

An ontology is dismantled by deleting the corresponding subschema in every participating co-database schema. In addition, all objects that belong to the classes of that ontology are also deleted. The update of co-databases resulting from inter-ontology relationship changes is practically the same as defined for ontologies. The only difference being that changes in ontologies obey a stricter set of rules.

2.5 WebFINDIT – An Ontology-based Architecture for Web Databases

This section presents the overall architecture that supports the WebFINDIT frame-work. This architecture adopts a client-server approach to provide services for interconnecting a large number of distributed, autonomous and heterogeneous databases [24, 26, 25]. It is based on *CORBA* and *Java* technologies. CORBA provides a robust object infrastructure for implementing distributed applications including multidatabase systems [77]. These applications are constructed seamlessly from their components (e.g., legacy systems or new developed systems) that are hosted on different locations on the network and developed using different programming languages and operating systems [12]. Interoperability across multi-vendor CORBA ORBs is provided by using IIOP (Internet Inter-ORB Protocol). The use of IIOP allows objects distributed over the Internet and connected to different ORBs to communicate. Java allows user interfaces to be deployed dynamically over the Web. Java applets can be downloaded onto the user machine and used to communicate with WebFINDIT components (e.g., CORBA objects). In addition, JDBC can be used to access SQL relational databases from Java applications. Java and CORBA offer complementary functionalities to develop and deploy distributed applications.

It should be noted that there are other types of middleware technologies besides Java/CORBA [15] [41]. Other technologies such as HTTP/CGI approach and ActiveX/DCOM [71] [12] are also used for developing intranet- and Internet-based applications. It is recognized that the HTTP/CGI approach may be adequate when there is no need for sophisticated remote server capabilities and no data sharing among databases is required. Otherwise, Java/CORBA approach offers several advantages over HTTP/CGI [41]. We note also that the CORBA's IIOP and HTTP can run on the same network as both of them uses the Internet as the backbone. Also, the interoperability between CORBA and ActiveX/DCOM is already a reality with the beta-version of Orbix COMet Desktop. Thus, the access to Internet databases interfaced using the CGI/HTML or ActiveX/DCOM will be possible at a minimal cost.

2.5.1 System Architecture of WebFINDIT

The WebFINDIT components are grouped into four layers that interact among themselves to query a large number of heterogeneous and distributed databases using a Web-based interface (see Figure 2.5). The basic components of WebFINDIT are the *query layer*, the *communication layer*, the *metadata layer*, and the *data layer*.

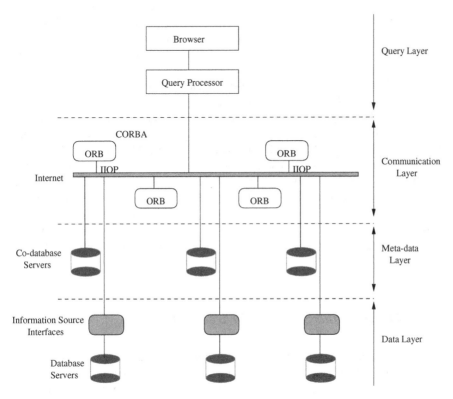

Fig. 2.5 WebFINDIT Multilayered Architecture

The query layer: provides users' access to WebFINDIT services. It has two components: The *browser* and the *query processor*. The browser is the user's interface to WebFINDIT. It uses the metadata stored in the co-databases to help users learn about the available information space, locate the information source servers, send query to remote databases and display their results. The browser is implemented using Java applets. The query processor receives queries from the browser, coordinates their execution and returns their results to the browser. The query processor interacts with the communication layer (next layer) which dispatches WebTassili queries to the co-databases (metadata layer) and databases (data layer). The query processor is written in Java.

The communication layer: manages the interaction between WebFINDIT components. It mediates requests between the query processor and co-database/database servers. The communication layer locates the set of servers that can perform the tasks. This component is implemented using a network of IIOP compliant CORBA ORBs, namely, VisiBroker for Java, OrbixWeb, and Orbix. By using CORBA, it is possible to encapsulate services (i.e., co-database and database servers) as sets of distributed objects and associated operations. These objects provide interfaces to access servers. The query processor communicates with CORBA ORBs either directly when the ORB is a client/server Java ORB (e.g., VisiBroker) or via another Java ORB (e.g., using OrbixWeb to communicate with Orbix).

The metadata layer: consists of a set of co-database servers that store metadata about the associated databases (i.e, information type, location, ontologies, inter-ontology relationships, and so on). Co-databases are designed to respond to queries regarding available information space and locating sources of an information type. All co-databases are implemented using XML as supported by Oracle.

The data layer: has two components: databases and Information Source Interfaces (ISIs). The current version of WebFINDIT supports relational (mSQL, Oracle, Sybase, DB2) and object oriented (ObjectStore) databases. An information source interface provides access to a specific database server. The current implementation of WebTassili provides : (1) translation of WebTassili queries to the native local language (e.g., SQL), (2) translation of results from the format of the native system to the format of WebTassili.

2.5.2 Hardware and Software Environment

The current implementation of our system is based on Solaris (v2.6), JDK (v1.1.5) which includes JDBC (v2.0) (used to access the relational databases), three CORBA products that are IIOP compliant, namely Orbix (v2), OrbixWeb (v3), and VisiBroker (v3.2) for Java (see Figure 2.6). These ORBs connect 26 databases (databases and their co-databases). Each database is encapsulated in a CORBA server object (a proxy). These databases are implemented using four different DBMSs (relational and object-oriented systems): Oracle, mSQL, DB2, and ObjectStore. The user interface is implemented as Java applets that communicate with CORBA objects. ObjectStore databases are connected to Orbix. Relational databases (stored in Oracle, mSQL, and DB2) are connected to a Java-interfaced CORBA. Oracle databases are connected to VisiBroker, whereas mSQL and DB2 are connected to OrbixWeb. CORBA server objects use:

- JDBC to communicate with relational databases. In this case, the CORBA objects are implemented in Java (OrbixWeb or VisiBroker for Java server objects).

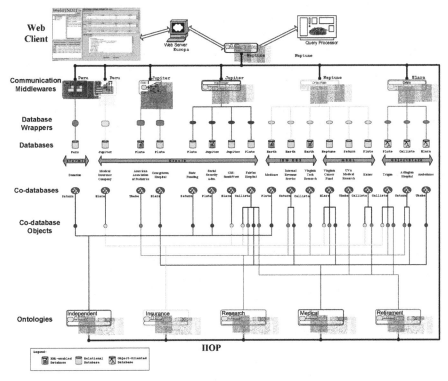

Fig. 2.6 Detailed Implementation of WebFINDIT

- C++ method invocation to communicate with C++ interfaced object-oriented databases from C++ CORBA servers (both Orbix and ObjectStore support C++ interface).

Chapter 3
Web Services Query Model

The basic use of Web services consists of invoking operations by sending and receiving messages. Their definition does not describe potential interactions between operations within the same Web service or other Web services. However, complex applications accessing diverse Web services (e.g., benefits for senior citizens) require advanced capabilities to manipulate and deliver Web services' functionalities. In general, users have needs that cannot be fulfilled by simply invoking one single operation or several operations independently.

As Web services are starting to get deployed on the Web, a large number of those Web services would compete by offering "similar" functionalities (e.g., different meals providers in the senior citizens scenario, different airlines offering the same connection between two cities.) However, they are expected to differ in the way that these functionalities are offered, e.g., required input and output parameters, and the conditions to use them, i.e., quality of Web services. In addition, satisfying users' requests may not necessarily require returning exact answers. Indeed, users may be satisfied by "alternative" or "partial" answers.

As a major step in addressing the above challenges, we propose a new approach to query Web services and the information flow generated during the invocation of their operations [74, 73]. Given a query, its resolution would lead to the invocation of various Web service operations and the combination of their results. The proposed query model enables users to express their requests through simple declarative queries. It is then incumbent on the query infrastructure supporting this model to efficiently transform this query into the best combination of invocations of actual Web service operations.

metrics to characterize *QoWS* and devise techniques to use it

As part of this query model, we define a comprehensive model for *QoWS* in the context of Web services [74]. We define *QoWS* parameters for individual Web services and for service execution plans composed of several Web services. Since *QoWS* parameters may be subject to various fluctuations during a Web service's life time, we propose a monitoring scheme that would assess *QoWS* advertised by service providers based on their actual behavior.

3.1 Three-Level Service Query Model

By drawing an analogy with databases, we propose a three-level query model for
Web services [74]. At the top level, we define *relations* that allows users to easily
formulate queries. At the second level, we define *virtual operations* specific to a
given application domain. They are termed "virtual" since they do not belong to any
actual Web service. The third level represents *concrete operations* from actual Web
services. The three-level model acts as a schema for the service space for querying
purposes. Although we build our Web service query model using database concepts,
we should note that there are few major differences. In databases, the actual data is
well known, static, and owned and managed by a central authority. In contrast, the
Web service query infrastructure needs to locate appropriate Web services for each
query. These *a priori* unknown and highly volatile Web services are independent
entities that compete against each other. In addition, in the proposed model, the
same query may be answered by different Web services if executed twice.

More precisely, the three-level query model is defined as follows:

- *Query Level* – Consists of a set of relations that allow users to formulate and
  submit declarative queries over Web services. Different sets of relations may be
  defined over the virtual operations using different mapping rules. This means that
  we may have different query interfaces depending on users' needs.

  Definition 3.1. $\mathscr{R}$ is a set of relations R_i defined at the query level. $\square$

  Examples of relations in the social services for a senior citizen application include *transportation options*, and *food provider menu*.
- *Virtual Level* – Consists of Web service-like operations typically offered in a
  particular application domain. They determine, along with the relations, the kind
  of queries that are supported by the query infrastructure.

  Definition 3.2. $\mathscr{V}$ is a set of virtual operations defined at the virtual level. $\square$

  Examples of virtual operations in the social services for a senior citizen application includes *Transportation. LegalAid*, and *MealsProvider*.
- *Concrete Level* – Represents the space of Web services offered on the Web.
  These are the potential candidates to answer queries. Web services are *a priori*
  unknown. They need to be discovered and matched with the virtual operations
  appearing in a query.

  Definition 3.3. $\mathscr{S}$ is the set of concrete operations from available Web services.
  It forms the concrete level. $\square$

A general scenario for the use of the three-level query model would be of a
"designer" willing to provide query capabilities over Web services in the senior
citizens scenario. Based on that target application, the designer starts by building
a set of virtual operations. Virtual operations represent basic operations that self-
sufficiency workers and senior citizens need to deal with in an area aging agency.
An important feature of the virtual operations is that they are not related *priori*

to any existing Web services. This is crucial since Web services are continuously evolving and the system is always looking for the best deals for users' queries. Next, the designer defines a set of relations. These relations are tailored for a particular user group that is interested in some specific part of the service space (by adding conditions, composing virtual operations, etc.) For example, citizens will not have access to the same set of virtual operations as self-sufficiency workers. Finally, users would pose queries using those relations.

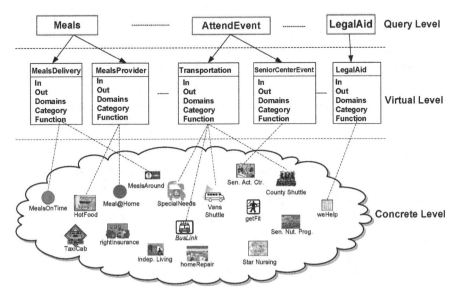

Fig. 3.1 The Three-Level Query Scheme for the Senior Citizens Scenario

In Figure 3.1, we illustrate the three level scheme for the senior citizens scenario. For example, the self-sufficiency worker could get services for providing meals in a given area and fulfilling some conditions (price, quantity, etc.) by simply formulating a query that uses the relation *Meals*. This relation is then mapped to its corresponding virtual operations *DeliverMeal* and *PrepareMeal*. Each of these virtual operations could then be matched to various operations from the concrete level. For example, *DeliverMeal* could be matched to operations from two potential Web services MealsOnTime and FoodAround (Figure 3.1).

3.1.1 Mapping Relations to Virtual Operations

Relations at the query level define a specific view of the application domain. They are obtained by invoking one or several virtual operations. We represent them as conjunctive queries over virtual operations. This is as if the virtual operations were viewed as relations. More precisely, let $\mathscr{R}$ be the set of relations defined at the query level and $\mathscr{VOP}$ the set of virtual operations.

Definition 3.4. For any relation $R_i \in \mathscr{R}$,

$$R_i(x_1, x_2, ..., x_n) \; :- \; \bigwedge_j Vop_j(y_{j_1}, ..., y_{j_m}), \bigwedge_k C_k$$

where x_i are the attributes of R_i, $Vop_j \in \mathscr{VOP}$, and y_j are input and output variables of the corresponding operation. C_k's represent conditions on variables appearing in the different virtual operations Vop_j. Their form is: $C_k = x \; op \; c$, where x is an input or output variable from any Vop_j, c a constant, and $op \in \{=, \neq, <, >, \geq, \leq\}$. $\square$

The :- is the transcription of an implication arrow. It means that to get R_i, we need to invoke the different operations Vop_j. The part before the :- is referred to as *head*, the part after :- as *body*. The $\bigwedge$ refers to a conjunction and is usually replaced by a comma sign. Multiple occurrences of a variable express equality. Different sets of relations could be defined at the query level using the same set of virtual operations. Our definition of relations as conjunction of operations does not mandate any order on their invocation. The order will be obtained during the processing and optimization phase of complete queries. This enables more flexibility in deciding which Web services to use to solve the query. An example of a mapping rule is:

> *Meals*(Zipcode, MealType, MealPrice, DeliveryPrice) :-
>   *DeliverMeals*(*Area, DeliveryPrice*),
>   *PrepareMeals*(*ProviderZip, MealType, MealPrice*),
>   *Zipcode* $\in$ *Area*,
>   *ProviderZip* $\in$ *Area*

The view relation *Meals* is defined through two virtual operations: *DeliverMeals* returns a meals delivery service operating in a certain area and *PrepareMeals* returns a meals providers. *Area* is a list of zipcodes where the delivery service operates. The mapping rule states conditions to make sure that the meal delivery service serves an area that includes both the meal provider and the zipcode specified in the relation.

Users may directly use virtual operations to access Web services. However, the use of relations has two benefits: It allows the definition of a natural way to formulate and submit (database-like) queries through the concept of relations that can be assimilated to relations in databases. In addition, it provides a view tailored for a particular group of users interested in some specific part of the service space.

3.2 Virtual Operations Representation

For any virtual operation appearing in a query, we need to locate the relevant concrete operation from an *a priori* unknown service space. Matching between virtual and concrete operations must occur in a fully automated way. The description of virtual operations should contain enough information to decide if a match is possible. In the same time, it should be flexible enough to allow a wide range of concrete operation selections. For that purpose, a semantic description is required in addition to syntactic attributes.

We assume that business partners would agree on a *common ontology*. This common ontology is used in the description of concrete Web services and virtual operations. The ontology-based description of Web services described in [59, 60] is adopted. This ontology has been specified using DAML+OIL [52]. We assume that each operation, either virtual or concrete, is semantically described through its *Category* and *Function*. *Function* contains two attributes: *functionality* and *synonyms*. The functionality represents the business functionality provided by the operation. Examples of functionalities include *eligibility screening* and *listing*. The synonyms attribute contains a list of alternative functionality names for the operation. For example, *eligibility screening* is synonym of *eligibility check*. *Category* contains also two attributes: *domain* and *synonyms*. The domain gives the area of interest of the operation. Examples of domains include *food*, *legal*, and *counseling*. Synonyms attributes are similar to those defined for the operation's purpose.

Another important aspect for Web services is that to be able to invoke any operation, it is necessary to provides values for its input variables. In formulating queries, users are free to specify any type of conditions on the different variables. This may lead to a scenario where the system cannot invoke operations due to missing values for some input variables. We propose to specify as part of virtual operation descriptions all possible values (range) of some of their input variables (this may not always be possible for all input variables). This means that during query processing, an input variable with a range is expanded into all its possible values depending on the condition in which it is involved.

Operations have variables that play either the role of input or output. There may be situations where Web services offering similar functionalities use the same variable as input in some of these Web services and output in others. For example, two transportation services may specify a variable related to pricing type (per use, per ride, monthly, etc.) as an input in one case and output in another. As a way to enhance the flexibility of virtual operations in allowing more possible concrete operations matches, we propose to define variables that can be either input or output. Only at processing time, when actual Web services are located and matched against virtual operations, that the actual nature (input or output) of those variables is determined.

Definition 3.5. Each virtual operation is formally represented by a quintuple

$$Vop = (In, Out, InOut, Domains, Category, Function)$$

where *In* is the set of input variables, *Out* the set of output variables, *InOut* the set variables that may be either input or output, *Domains* a set of pair $(x, range)$ where x is an enumerable variable appearing in *In* and *range* is the set of all possible values for *x*, *Category* describes the domain of interest, and *Function* describes the business function. □

The following is an example of a virtual operation with all of its attributes:

$$TransportationOptions \; = \; (In, Out, InOut, Domains, Category, Function)$$

where *In* = (DepartureZip, ArrivalZip), *Out* = (Rules, PricingType, Price), *InOut* = ∅, *Domains*= ∅, *Category* = {Travel, Transportation}, and *Function* = {Listing, Fares}.

3.2.1 Service Queries Specification

Queries are formulated using *relations* from the query level. Usually, users pose their queries through some user-friendly graphical user interface. However, queries are manipulated internally in the query infrastructure as conjunctive queries.

Definition 3.6. Q is a conjunctive (select-project-join) query over $\mathscr{R}$. Its general form is

$$Q(X) \; :- \; \bigwedge_i R_i(X_{i_1}), \bigwedge_k C_k$$

R_i are relations from the query level. X and X_i are tuples of variables such that $\forall x \in X$, $\exists x \in X_i$. C_k's represent conditions on variables appearing in the query. Their form is: $C_k = x \; op \; c$, where x is an input or output variable appearing in any X_i, c a constant, and $op \in \{=, \neq, <, >, \geq, \leq\}$. □

To illustrate the use of our query model and how a given need for information and services is expressed using simple declarative queries, we present some examples from the senior citizens scenario. Without loss of generality, the different operations are expressed directly over virtual operations. A query bearing over relations is easily transformed into a query bearing on virtual operations by simply applying the different mapping rules defined in the application. Table 3.1 outlines a sample of virtual operations that could be defined for a senior citizen application.

Let us now present different potential queries that Maria or the self-sufficiency worker may submit. For example, Maria is looking for the best Web services for a transportation service and an art gallery service. She may submit either two different queries for each service or one single query for both even if the two do not need to be necessarily invoked together. In the latter case, she may take advantage of some potential discounts that may be offered by an art gallery in partnership with a transportation service.

- Individual selection of Web services (Figure 3.2).

    Query₁(Rules, PricingType, Price) :-
            Transportation(DepartureZip, ArrivalZip, Rules, PricingType, Price),

Table 3.1 Examples of Virtual Operations in the Senior Citizens Scenario

Operation	Input	Output	Comment
Transportation	DepartureZip, ArrivalZip	Rules, PricingType, Price	Get transportation services provided between two zip codes. The returned information includes the rules for using the service, the price, and the pricing policy (e.g., per ride, per month, etc.)
ArtGallery	Zipcode	OperationHours	Provide information about an art gallery in a given zip code
PrepareMeal	ProviderZip	MealType, MealPrice	It returns type and price of meals for food providers in a given zip code
DeliverMeal	Area	DeliveryPrice	Provides delivery services in a given area.
GroupTransportation	OriginatingZipCode	Price, ServedArea, Capacity	Provides group transportation
ActivityCenter	Zipcode	OperationHours	Provides hours of operation of an activity center

Price<30, DepartureZip=22044, ArrivalZip=22311
Query₂(Zipcode, OperationHours) :-
    ArtGallery(Zipcode, OperationHours),
    Zipcode=22311

Fig. 3.2 Individual Selection of Web Services

- Combined selection of Web services (Figure 3.3).

    Query(Rules, PricingType, Price, Zipcode, OperationHours) :-
        Transportation(DepartureZip, ArrivalZip, Rules, PricingType, Price),
        ArtGallery(Zipcode, OperationHours),
        Price<30, DepartureZip=22044, ArrivalZip=22311, Zipcode=22311

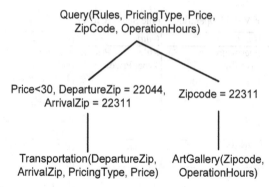

Query(Rules, PricingType, Price,
ZipCode, OperationHours)

Price<30, DepartureZip = 22044,   Zipcode = 22311
ArrivalZip = 22311

Transportation(DepartureZip,   ArtGallery(Zipcode,
ArrivalZip, PricingType, Price)   OperationHours)

Fig. 3.3 Combined Selection of Web Services

In another example, Maria is looking for the best "combination" of Web services to meet her nutritional needs (Figure 3.4). Combined selection of Web services needs to take into account potential relationships.

Query(Zipcode, MealType, MealPrice, DeliveryPrice) :-
PrepareMeal(ProviderZip, MealType, MealPrice),
DeliverMeal(Area, DeliveryPrice),
MealPrice + DeliveryPrice < $15,
Zipcode ∈ Area,
ProviderZip ∈ Area,
Zipcode = 22043

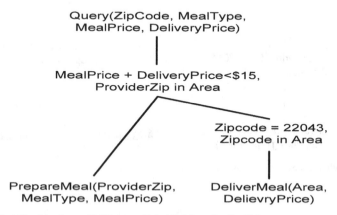

Query(ZipCode, MealType,
MealPrice, DeliveryPrice)

MealPrice + DeliveryPrice<$15,
ProviderZip in Area

Zipcode = 22043,
Zipcode in Area

PrepareMeal(ProviderZip,   DeliverMeal(Area,
MealType, MealPrice)   DelievryPrice)

Fig. 3.4 Best Combination with Discount Relationships - Senior Citizen

Let us assume now that the self-sufficiency worker is looking for the best providers for carrying a group of senior citizens to a specific event in a certain activity center (Figure 3.5).

Query(Price, ServedArea, Capacity, OperationHours) :-
      GroupTransportation(OriginatingZipCode, Price, ServedArea, Capacity),
      ActivityCenter(Zipcode, OperationHours),
      Price<$50,
      OriginatingZipCode=22018,
      OriginatingZipCode $\in$ ServedArea,
      Zipcode = 22044,
      Zipcode $\in$ ServedArea,
      capacity > 25

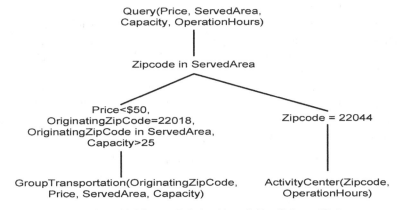

Fig. 3.5 Best Combination with Discount Relationships - Self-sufficiency Worker

3.2.1.1 Specifying Post-Conditions in Queries

Users could *a priori* specify any kind of conditions in their queries. Generally, these conditions can only be checked after one or more related operations have been invoked. The non fulfillment of a condition by some specific Web services does not mean necessarily that there are no other Web services that can fulfill it. Thus, we may need to lookup for concrete operations for a given virtual operation and invoke them several times before getting the right match, i.e., the concrete operation that meets the conditions. Examples of such conditions may concern capacity and price of a transportation service, hours of operation of a food provider, delivery time for certain goods, and so on.

We should also note that in some situations, the non fulfillment of a post-condition may not require to look for another Web service. This includes the following situations:

- Unique match – The virtual operation was matched to one single concrete operation.
- Invariable outcome – The outcome will be the same regardless of which concrete operation is being used.
- User requirement – The user sets a limit of one invocation per virtual operation.

3.2.2 Multi-level Matching for Virtual Operations

Following the fast proliferation of Web services, different providers are expected to compete in their offerings. They would offer "similar" functionalities but differently. Differences may occur in the required input, returned output, quality of service, etc. This also means that it is not always possible to find an exact match for a given virtual operation. In addition, users may be willing to accept similar or close answers. Thus, instead of trying to only find concrete operations that match exactly virtual operations appearing in a query, we propose a more flexible matching scheme where virtual and concrete operations' attributes may differ. This scheme generates different levels of *precision* for the matching process.

We define a function *similar* to check whether two attributes appearing in two operations are the same. $similar(x,y)$ is *True* if x and y correspond to the same concepts with respect to the common ontology defined in the application domain. For any two operations op_1 and op_2, $In(op_1) = In(op_2)$ if

- (i) $In(op_1)$ and $In(op_2)$ have the same number of variables and
- (ii) $\forall x \in In(op_1)$ (resp. $In(op_2)$), $\exists y \in In(op_2)$ (resp. $In(op_1)$) $|$ $similar(x,y)$ is *True*.

$Out(op_1) = Out(op_2)$ is defined similarly. We also define $In(op_1) \subset In(op_2)$ and $Out(op_1) \subset Out(op_2)$ in a similar way where the first set is a subset of the second set.

Let Vop and $Concop$ be two virtual and concrete operations respectively. We identified four different matching levels obtained by varying the way attributes of virtual and concrete operations are compared.

1. *Exact match* – The concrete operation matches the virtual operation with respect to all attributes. Two operations match *exactly* if they have the same input and output variables, and the same *Category* and *Function* respectively.
2. *Overlapping match* – Relates to an operation offering *close* functionalities to that of the virtual operation. Two operations *overlap* if they have the same input and output variables, and their *Category* and *Function* (as defined in the common ontology) overlap.
3. *Partial match* – Corresponds to the case where input and output attributes of the two operations do not coincide. Two operations Vop and $Concop$ match *partially* if they have the same *Category* and *Function* respectively, and $Out(Concop) \subseteq Out(Vop)$ or $In(Concop) \subseteq In(Vop)$, An example for the first subset relationship

is an operation that does not return all the output attributes expected by the virtual operation.

4. *Partial and overlap match* – This level is a combination of the *overlap* and *partial* matches. Two operations Vop and $Concop$ match *partially* and by *overlap* if $Out(Concop) \subseteq Out(Vop)$ or $In(Concop) \subseteq In(Vop)$ and their $Category$ and $Function$ attributes overlap.

We assign a *matching degree* to each level. This quantifies the precision of the matching. The *matching degree* has a direct impact on the quality of the query results. We compute the *matching degree* for any matched concrete operation based on the matching level. We define four matching degrees for the above levels respectively: 1, $9/10$, $8/10$, and $7/10$. These values are arbitrary. Their main goal is to distinguish the different matching levels. They may be changed depending on the intended impact of these degrees on the optimization process.

3.2.3 Three-level Model Reconfiguration

As the system evolves, the definition of the different entities constituting the "service schema" may be fine tuned to better reflect users' needs. This is especially the case for the definition of virtual operations. Indeed, the service space is highly volatile, Web services and their operations may be subject to frequent changes due to market fluctuations, changes in regulations, and to maintain competitive advantage. This may lead to virtual operations that cannot be matched to any concrete operation through any of the matching levels that we have defined. Also, new "interesting" Web services may be available. However, their (concrete) operations cannot be matched to existing virtual operations in any way. In addition, relations and mapping rules may not properly serve users. Due constraints such as expanding and diversifying users' needs, new regulations, users may need different or more relations.

To support such evolution of the system, we propose a semi-automatic reconfiguration of the three-level model. This is mainly based on collecting information on failed queries, partial and overlap matches, and poor quality service execution plans. The collected information can be used by the service schema designer to modify one or more of those entities. We also collect usage patterns and users' feedback on the use of our system to suggest changes at the query level. Here are few events that may trigger a change in the three-level query model. A virtual operation has not been used for a long time period. A large number of queries using some specific relations or virtual operations never succeed.

3.3 Quality of Web Service Model

The concept of quality of service has been mostly used in the context of networking and multimedia applications. In [93], quality of service is defined as the "collective effect of service performance, which determines the satisfaction of a user of a service. It is characterized by the combined aspects of performance factors applicable to all services". To a certain extent, this definition holds also in the context of our query infrastructure. However, in the case of Web services, we need to go beyond classical system-centric quality. Different aspects that influence the user experience with the Web service should be taken into account. In this section, we define different *QoWS* parameters for Web services and service execution plans and categorize them based on the behavioral aspects they characterize.

3.3.1 Quality of Web Service Parameters

We assume that each Web service would advertise its *QoWS* parameters in a service registry. Not all parameters would be applicable to all types of Web services. In addition, some parameters may be either computed by the query infrastructure or obtained from third parties (e.g., rating systems like epinions.com that could be used for the *reputation* parameter). The way that these parameters are specified is beyond the scope of this work. Our focus is on defining those parameters and using them in the context of optimization.

Definition 3.7. *QoWS* of a Web service is a vector of *QoWS* parameters. A *QoWS* parameter is defined by a couple: QoWSp = (Name, Value). Name is the name of the *QoWS* parameter. Value could be *NA* if the parameter is not applicable for the Web service or its value cannot be obtained. This value may represent a probability, a scalar ($\Re^+$), or an enumeration. □

We assume that the meaning of the *QoWS* parameters is common to all Web services. A *QoWS* could be generic enough to be used across domains or application specific. For example, response time or latency are inherent to any operation invocation. However, a transportation service could be characterized with its *on time rate*. This is clearly not applicable to any Web service. In our work, we focus on generic parameters. However, our model is easily extensible to include other application specific parameters. We consider two main categories of generic *QoWS* depending on the behavior of the Web service they characterize: *computational behavior* and *business behavior* (Figure 3.6).

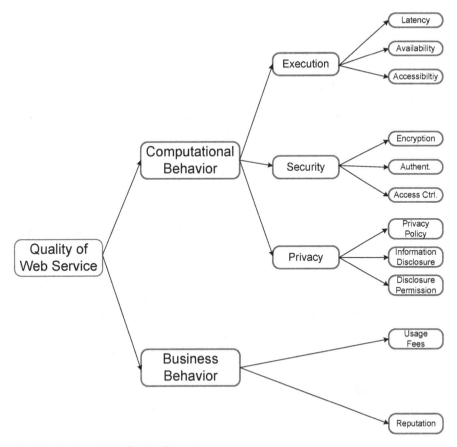

Fig. 3.6 Quality of Web Service Categories

Computational QoWS

Computational *QoWS* characterizes various aspects related to invoking Web service operations as perceived by the service consumer. It is further organized into three sub-categories:

- Execution – Includes performance parameters while interacting with the Web service. We consider the following parameters:

  - *Latency* – Latency represents the average time for an operation to return results after its invocation.
  - *Availability* – It represents the probability that a service is available. Large values mean high availability. Small values indicate low availability. Availability is defined in [89] as the property that a system is ready to be used

immediately. In general, it refers to the probability that the system is operating at any given moment and is available to perform its functions on behalf of its users. In other words, a highly available system is one that will most likely be working at a given instant in time.

- *Accessibility* – It represents the degree that a Web service is capable of serving a request. It may be measured by the ratio between the number of requests being sent to the Web service and the number of requests that are effectively served. There could be situations when a Web service is available but not accessible.

- *Security* – Relates to the ability of the Web service in providing appropriate security mechanisms. The following parameters are considered (they are equal to 0 or 1):

  - *Encryption* – Whether the Web service supports encryption of messages (received and sent).
  - *Authentication* – Whether the Web service provides mechanisms to identify the invoking party (i.e., service consumer) and allow operation invocation.
  - *Access control* – Whether the Web service supports access control by restricting operation invocation and access to information to authorized parties.

- *Privacy* – Relates to the ability of the Web service in preserving privacy of submitted information. This includes the following parameters that are equal to 0 or 1.

  - *Privacy policy* – Specifies whether the Web service has a privacy policy.
  - *Information sharing* – Specifies whether the Web services shares collected information with third parties.
  - *Information disclosure* – Specifies whether the Web service asks for explicit permission to disclose information to third parties.

Business QoWS

Business *QoWS* includes the following parameters:

- *Usage Fee* – It represents units of money that a consumer of a Web service needs to pay to use the Web service, i.e., invoke operations.
- *Reputation* – Measures the reputation of the Web services based on user feedbacks. Users are prompted to rate Web services on a [1, 10] scale after the end of a querying session. The reputation corresponds to the average of collected ratings.

The previous parameters can be also be classified as being either *negative* or *positive* parameters. In negative parameters, the higher the value, the worse the quality. They include latency and usage fees. In positive parameters, the lower the value, the worse the quality. They include availability, accessibility, reliability, authentication, encryption, access control, privacy policy, information sharing, information disclosure, and reputation. Table 3.2 summarizes the different *QoWS* parameters.

Table 3.2 Quality of Web Service Summary

Category	Sub-Category	Parameter	Definition	Potential values
Computational	Execution	Latency	Average response time	scalar $\Re^+$
		Availability	Probability that the Web service is ready for immediate use	[0, 1]
		Accessibility	Ratio between served and received requests	[0, 1]
	Security	Encryption	Support or not message encryption	[0, 1]
		Authentication	Support or not authentication of invoking party	{0, 1}
		Access control	Restrict or not operation invocation and information access	{0, 1}
	Privacy	Privacy policy	Provide or not a privacy policy	{0, 1}
		Information sharing	Share or not collected information	{0, 1}
		Information disclosure	Ask or not for permission to disclose information	{0, 1}
Business		Usage Fee	Cost of invoking operations	scalar $\Re^+$
		Reputation	Reputation obtained from user feedbacks	[0, 10]

3.3.2 Discount Relationships for Combined Use of Web Services

In an era of high competition and shared interests, it is often the case that different service providers would engage in partnerships. These partnerships are usually translated by offering some privileges to customers that would use both partners in achieving some needs. In the case of our query infrastructure, this means that a user would get a "better" *QoWS* if a query is resolved by using two specific Web services. For example, in the scenario presented in the introduction, caring for the nutritional needs of Maria required three types of services *meals provider*, *meals delivery*, and *senior nutrition program*. In this case, individual providers for each type should be selected in a way that optimizes their combination. For instance, the choice of Meal@Home as a *meals provider* may reduce costs if combined with MealsOnTime as the *meals delivery* provider. These two providers are in business partnership to provide discounts for their common customers. This concept is captured by the following definition.

Definition 3.8. If a service provider SP_1 has a *discount relationship* with a service provider SP_2, $discount(SP_1, SP_2)$, then $\exists QoWS$ parameter P_i of SP_1, $P_i = discount *$ dv if SP_1 and SP_2 are both used to solve a query. dv is the default value for the parameter P_i. $0 < discount < 1$ if P_i is a negative parameter and $discount > 1$ if P_i is a positive parameter. (In both cases, the new values is better.) $\square$

A given service provider may be engaged in more than one *discount relationship*. In this case, the best discounted value for its *QoWS* parameter would be used if more than one partner is involved in resolving a given query. Without loss of generality, we assume that the *discount relationship* is non-symmetric. The value of the discount is decided by the partners and is advertised along the corresponding *QoWS* in the service registry.

3.4 Web Services Monitoring

Web services are dynamic and independent entities offering miscellaneous functionalities on the Web. For a given functionality, several Web services may compete in their offerings. The key difference would be on how these functionalities are to be delivered in terms of *QoWS*. However getting the right value for a given *QoWS* parameter is neither an easy nor a trivial task. In that context, monitoring Web services behavior would be crucial in either calculating *QoWS* parameters values or assessing a Web service claim in terms of promised *QoWS* [74]. The objective of the monitoring is to *rate* the behavior of the Web service in delivering its functionalities in terms of every *QoWS* parameter.

Monitoring may take different forms depending of the *QoWS* parameter. These include *message interception*, *probing*, and *user feedback*. To allow probing, we assume that Web services support some "free" operations that can be invoked without any effect for the invoker. Ideally, Web services should support a "ping" operation. To avoid a high overhead on the system, monitoring is conducted periodically. Finally, not all *QoWS* can be subjected to monitoring due to their nature or some limitations (we will explain the reason for each one of them).

3.4.1 Monitoring Process

Rating Web services require collecting different information depending on the *QoWS* being considered.

Execution Parameters Monitoring

- *Latency* – Actual latency values are collected during operation invocation and their average is computed over a given time period θ_{lat}.
- *Availability* – The Web service is pinged periodically. Failed and succeeded pings are recorded for a given time period θ_{av}. The ratio is calculated and recorded values are discarded.

- *Accessibility* – Number of successful and failed operation invocations are accumulated. Their ratio is computed for a given time period θ_{acc} and collected values are discarded.

Security Parameters Monitoring

The idea is to to detect if there is any security breach in terms of these parameters. If the Web service does not make any claim with regards to these parameters then it does not have to be monitored. Usually, operations should be invoked with proper security credentials. However, there may be cases where such requirement is violated.

- *Encryption* – The occurrence of any successful operation invocation with unencrypted messages is recorded. The average number of such occurrences is computed over a given time period θ_{enc}.
- *Authentication* – Any successful operation invocation without proper authentication is recoded. The average number of such occurrences is computed over a given time period θ_{aut}.
- *Access control* – Any successful invocation of restricted operations is recorded. The average number of such occurrences is computed over a given time period θ_{act}.

Privacy Parameters Monitoring

Privacy parameters may not be easily monitored by looking at individual operation invocation or probing Web services. We need to determine if a Web service violated its claims in terms of privacy parameters. Finding out about these violations require complex mechanisms similar to those described in [79]. Using such mechanisms is beyond the scope of our work. Below, we just briefly describe what needs to be checked.

- *Privacy policy* – The adherence of the Web service to the content of the privacy policy should be monitored.
- *Information sharing* – We need to find out whether the Web service disclosed information to third parties.
- *Information disclosure* – We need to find out whether the Web service disclosed information to third parties without proper permissions.

Business QoWS

- *Usage Fee* – The usage fee does not generally change from the published value and the actual value at invocation time. However, there may be cases where this may happen. In this case, we compute the difference between these two values.

- *Reputation* – This parameter is computed by the query infrastructure itself. It is not subject to monitoring.

The value of the different time periods $\theta_{<p_i>}$ and the frequency of the different information collections depend mainly on the *QoWS* being monitored and the application domain. For example, the value of θ_{fee} should be long enough as changes in fees do not occur frequently. In addition, if the load on the query infrastructure is very high, short time periods may be sufficient for monitoring based on message interception (e.g., latency, accessibility). Table 3.3 summarizes how monitoring is conducted for each *QoWS* parameter.

Table 3.3 Quality of Web Service Monitoring

Sub-Category	Parameter	Methodology	Collected Information
Execution	Latency	Messages interception	Average of actual latencies μ_{lat}
	Availability	Probing through pinging	Ratio of successful pings over total number of pings ρ_{av}
	Accessibility	Messages interception	Ratio of successful invocations over total number of invocations ρ_{acc}
Security	Encryption	Messages interception	Average number of successful encryption breaches μ_{enc}
	Authentication	Messages interception	Average number of successful authentication breaches μ_{aut}
	Access control	Messages interception	Average number of successful access control breaches μ_{act}
Privacy	Privacy policy	Not applicable	Not applicable
	Information sharing	Not applicable	Not applicable
	Information disclosure	Not applicable	Not applicable
Business	Usage Fee	Values collection	Difference between advertised and requested fees
	Reputation	Not applicable	Not applicable

3.4.2 Rating Web Services

The general idea of rating Web services is to compute a *QoWS distance (QoWSdist)* for each *QoWS* parameter that quantifies the Web service behavior in delivering promised *QoWS*, *pQoWS*. This distance depends on: the *QoWS* meaning, whether the parameter is negative or positive, the advertised or promised value *pQoWS*, and the information being collected through monitoring. The value of this distance would be used to either increase or decrease the rating assigned to each *QoWS*. The following formulas give the *QoWSdist* for the parameters subject to monitoring.

$QoWSdist_{lat} = pQoWS_{lat} - \mu_{lat}$

$QoWSdist_{av} = \rho_{av} - pQoWS_{av}$

$QoWSdist_{acc} = \rho_{acc} - pQoWS_{acc}$

$QoWSdist_{enc} = \mu_{enc}$ if $pQoWS_{enc} = 1$

$QoWSdist_{aut} = \mu_{aut}$ if $pQoWS_{aut} = 1$

$QoWSdist_{act} = \mu_{act}$ if $pQoWS_{act} = 1$

$QoWSdist_{fee} = pQoWS_{fee} - dQoWS_{fee}$ ($dQoWS_{fee}$ is what is effectively requested)

Without loss of generality, we assume that ratings take values in the interval [0, 1]. For the sake of homogenization (and fairness), parameters not subject to monitoring are assigned a fixed rating which is is the highest value. Web services receive initially the highest ratings for all their $QoWS$. As the query infrastructure evolves and a $QoWSdist$ for a $QoWS$ is available, the corresponding rating is (re-)evaluated. The general idea is that whenever the $QoWSdist$ goes beyond certain thresholds the rating is either increased or decreased by a certain amount. This reflects how good or bad the Web service is behaving in terms of providing the promised $QoWS$. Note that any increase or decrease of a rating is bound by the maximum and minimum values 1 and 0. We summarize below how each rating is computed.

$$rat_{lat} = \begin{cases} max(rat_{lat} + \delta_{lat}, 1) & \text{if } QoWSdist_{lat} > \tau_{lat} > 0 \\ min(0, rat_{lat} - \delta_{lat}) & \text{if } QoWSdist_{lat} < -\tau_{lat} \end{cases}$$

$$rat_{av} = \begin{cases} max(rat_{av} + \delta_{av}, 1) & \text{if } QoWSdist_{av} > \tau_{av} > 0 \\ min(0, rat_{av} - \delta_{av}) & \text{if } QoWSdist_{av} < -\tau_{av} \end{cases}$$

$$rat_{acc} = \begin{cases} max(rat_{acc} + \delta_{acc}, 1) & \text{if } QoWSdist_{acc} > \tau_{acc} > 0 \\ min(0, rat_{acc} - \delta_{acc}) & \text{if } QoWSdist_{acc} < -\tau_{acc} \end{cases}$$

$$rat_{enc} = \begin{cases} max(rat_{enc} + \delta_{enc}, 1) & \text{if } QoWSdist_{enc} < \tau_{enc} \\ min(0, rat_{enc} - \delta_{enc}) & \text{if } QoWSdist_{enc} > \tau_{enc} > 0 \end{cases}$$

$$rat_{aut} = \begin{cases} max(rat_{aut} + \delta_{aut}, 1) & \text{if } QoWSdist_{aut} < \tau_{aut} \\ min(0, rat_{aut} - \delta_{aut}) & \text{if } QoWSdist_{aut} > \tau_{aut} > 0 \end{cases}$$

$$rat_{act} = \begin{cases} max(rat_{act} + \delta_{act}, 1) & \text{if } QoWSdist_{act} < \tau_{act} \\ min(0, rat_{act} - \delta_{act}) & \text{if } QoWSdist_{act} > \tau_{act} > 0 \end{cases}$$

$$rat_{fee} = \begin{cases} max(rat_{fee} + \delta_{fee}, 1) & \text{if } QoWSdist_{fee} < \tau_{fee} \\ (min(0, rat_{fee} - \delta_{fee}) & \text{if } QoWSdist_{fee} > \tau_{fee} > 0 \end{cases}$$

Ratings will be mainly used to weigh the $QoWS$ in determining an optimal service execution plan. They play an important role in the objective function. Our rating scheme evolves in a way that privileges Web services that respect their promises in terms of $QoWS$. However, its dynamic nature gives a chance to Web services with low ratings to catch up. These Web services may improve their ratings by either changing their promised $QoWS$, putting more efforts to achieve them, or both.

3.4.3 Monitoring Fine Tuning

The proposed monitoring and the ratings it produces depend on several parameters. These include monitoring methods (e.g., message interception, and probing.) values collection policy, number of values collected, collection frequency, and threshold values for distance checks.

These parameters determine the aggressivity and degree of tolerance at which we would like to conduct monitoring and rating. Using a too aggressive approach (for example, by conducting frequent probing, allowing very small thresholds, etc.) may deliver more precise ratings. However, this may put an important burden on the query infrastructure that will need to spend more resources rating Web services than serving its users. A tolerant approach will put less burden on the query infrastructure but delivers poor quality ratings. We could still follow such approach with some $QoWS$ parameters. For example, we may be tolerant in terms of availability but more reluctant to tolerate degradation of privacy or latency. A fair approach would be to have a configurable monitoring approach. In this case, the different parameters are adjusted depending on the requirements, in terms of rating precision, of the application being used.

Chapter 4
Web Services Query Execution and Optimization

In the previous chapter, we introduced our new web service query model. Users express their requests using the specifications we introduced in the same chapter. Now given such a query and a large pool of Web services along with their *QoWS* parameters, we need to transform this query into an executable orchestration of actual web services.

Due to the large space of competing Web services, a query could be potentially solved by several service execution plans using different Web services. Thus, it is necessary to set appropriate criteria to select the "best" service execution plan amongst all possible. Recent literature [94, 37, 83] shows that *Quality of Service or Quality of Web Service* (QoWS) of individual Web services is crucial for their competitiveness. In addition, there is an increasing need to provide acceptable *QoWS* over Web applications. The concept of *QoWS* would capture more accurately users and applications' requirements for efficiency and hence for query optimization on the Web. The challenge is to define appropriate metrics to characterize *QoWS* and devise techniques to use it in optimizing service-based queries. In our approach, *QoWS* encompasses a number of quantitative and qualitative parameters (non-functional properties) that measure the Web service performance in delivering its functionalities [74, 73, 76]. We present several algorithms that optimize queries based on the proposed *QoWS* model and in the presence of different constraints. As we will see, these constraints make the task of finding the optimal service execution plan extremely challenging.

4.1 Web Services Execution Plan

Queries are expressed using relations from the query level. They will be subject to several transformations, outlined in Figure 4.1, until obtaining a service execution plan that contains concrete operations and the order in which they need to be invoked.

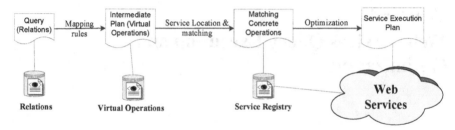

Fig. 4.1 Query Transformations

Answering a query requires accessing several Web services. Operation invocations may occur either in sequence or in parallel depending on potential constraints that may exist between the different operations. We represent a service execution plan by a directed graph. This allows to express sequence and concurrency of operation invocations.

Definition 4.1. A service execution plan *SEP* is represented by a directed graph $G = (V, E)$ called *execution graph*. $V = (op_s, op_t, OP)$ where *OP* is the set of operations being invoked by the service execution plan. op_s and op_t are two special nodes that do not correspond to any actual operation. They represent the starting and termination of *SEP*. *E* is a set of edges that represent the control flow of *SEP*. An edge will be drawn from a node op_i to a node op_j, if op_j has to be executed after op_i. Operations with no connecting paths can be executed concurrently. □

4.1.1 Web Services Operation Dependencies

Whenever an operation needs to be invoked, it is necessary to have all its input variables available or bound [74]. We capture this requirement by defining, for any operation, a *dependency* set containing all operations which output variables are used as input variables by that operation. For example, if $op_1(x^i, y^i, z^o), op_2(x^i, z^i, t^o)$, and $op_3(z^i, t^i, v^o)$ then $dependency(op_2) \supseteq \{op_1\}$ and $depedency(op_3) \supseteq \{op_1, op_2\}$. The notations x^i means that x is an input variable and z^o means that z is an output variable. Bound variables provided by the query are available to all operations. Operations that draw all their required input from bound variables specified in the query could be the first to be invoked in the service execution plan.

Definition 4.2. For any operation *op*, we define its *dependency set* as:
$dependency(op) = \{op_i / \exists x \in Output(op_i), x \in Input(op)\}$. □

Based on dependencies, we define a *dependency graph*, DG_Q for any query Q. This is a directed graph that is initially built based on binding requirements of virtual operations. As the query is processed, this graph is updated to reflect dependencies amongst concrete operations. With this graph we can easily know which operations are missing any input variable.

Definition 4.3. For any query Q, we define a dependency graph DG_Q. $DG_Q = (op_Q, op_\emptyset, V, E)$. op_Q represents a node acting as an operation which output variables are all the bindings provided initially by the query. $op_\emptyset$ represents a node acting as an operation that does not provide any output variable. Vertices in V are the different operations in the query Q including op_Q and $op_\emptyset$. Edges in E represent dependency relationships between operations. An edge is drawn from op_i to op_j if $op_i \in dependency(op_i)$. An edge is drawn from $op_\emptyset$ to op_i if op_i requires an input variable that is not provided by any other node in the graph. □

A straightforward use of dependency graphs is to check if a query is answerable or not based on binding requirements. For example, Figure 4.2 represents two dependency graphs: DG_{Q_1} may be answerable while DG_{Q_2} may not. Thus, if a query is found to be non answerable, we could instruct the service locator to match the corresponding virtual operation (with an edge to $op_\emptyset$) to a concrete operation that does not require the missing input variables. This may not lead to an exact answer for the query. However, such partial or close answers may be acceptable for the user.

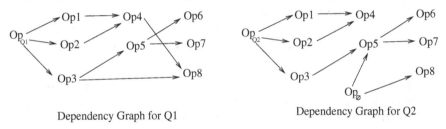

Dependency Graph for Q1   Dependency Graph for Q2

Fig. 4.2 Dependency Graphs

4.1.2 Feasibility of a Service Execution Plan

Although the main concern of the optimizer is to find the best service execution plan, it is necessary to make sure that the plan is effectively executable or *feasible*. In the context of our query infrastructure, we have to make sure that whenever an operation is ready to be invoked, all its output variables must be available and bound. In addition, if a Web service is selected based on its discounted $QoWS$, we need to make sure that its partner Web services are effectively being used in the resolution of the query. All of the above specify the conditions that need to be fulfilled to have a *feasible* service execution plan.

Definition 4.4. A service execution plan is *feasible* if (i) for any operation op_i in *SEP*, all required input bindings op_i are available when op_i is ready to be invoked, and (ii) if a Web service has been selected using a discounted *QoWS*, its partners in the discount relationship should be present in *SEP*. □

4.1.3 Quality of Web Service for Service Execution Plans

A given Web service ws_i is characterized by a vector of *QoWS* parameters,

$$QoWS(ws_i) = (lat(ws_i), av(ws_i), acc(ws_i), enc(ws_i), aut(ws_i), act(ws_i), \\ pp(ws_i), is(ws_i), id(ws_i), fee(ws_i), rep(ws_i)).$$

lat (latency) and *fee* (usage fee) take scalar values ($\Re^+$). *av* (availability), and *acc* (accessibility represent probability values (a real value between 0 and 1). *enc* (encryption), *aut* (authentication), *act* (access control), *pp* (privacy policy), *is* (information sharing), and *id* (information disclosure) are Boolean values (0 or 1). Finally, *rep* (reputation) ranges over the interval [0,10].

We need now to compute the *QoWS* parameters for the entire service execution plan. Based on the meaning of *QoWS*, we define the following aggregation functions to compute *QoWS* of service execution plans. We assume that Web services are independent with respect to their *QoWS*. This would allow to easily aggregate parameters representing a probability. We also assume that the service execution plan contains N operations.

- *Latency* – As some Web services may be accessed concurrently, we need to determine the longest path, with respect to latency, in the execution graph between the starting and ending nodes. The latency of the service execution plan corresponds to the sum of latencies of Web services being executed in sequence along this path.
- *Availability* – The service execution plan depends on the availability of all Web services it accesses. Thus, its availability corresponds to the probability that all Web services are available. As we assume that Web services are independent in terms of *QoWS* it is equal to $\prod_{i=1}^{N} av(ws_i)$.
- *Accessibility* – Accessibility is computed similarly to availability. It corresponds to the probability that all Web services are accessible: $\prod_{i=1}^{N} acc(ws_i)$.
- *Encryption* – This *QoWS* takes a Boolean value (0 or 1) for individual Web services. We could either assume that the service execution plan has a 0 value for encryption if at least one of the Web service has a 0 value, or we consider the ratio of encrypted Web services. Both options may be desirable. Thus, we leave it up to the user or the query infrastructure administrator to select which option to use.
- *Authentication* – This parameter is treated similarly to encryption.
- *Access control* – This parameter is treated similarly to encryption.
- *Privacy policy* – This parameter is treated similarly to encryption.
- *Information sharing* – This parameter is treated similarly to encryption.

- *Information disclosure* – This parameter is treated similarly to encryption.
- *Usage Fee* – Accessing all Web services appearing in the service execution plan requires paying access fees for all of them. This parameter corresponds to the sum of all usage fees of all invoked Web services: $\sum_{i=1}^{N} fee(ws_i)$.
- *Reputation* – The reputation of the service execution plan depends on the reputation of all its Web services. This parameter corresponds to the average of the reputation of all invoked Web services: $\frac{1}{N}\sum_{i=1}^{N} rep(ws_i)$.

Table 4.1 summarizes the different aggregation functions used to compute the *QoWS* parameters of a service execution plan.

4.2 Processing and Optimizing Web Service Queries

Selecting an optimal service execution plan is at the core of our query infrastructure. This challenging task is exacerbated by the large number of competing Web services that the optimizer would need to select from. Different service execution plans using different Web services could be used to solve the same query. However, they may differ according to the *QoWS* they deliver. These differences can be several orders of magnitude large. Thus, it is necessary to devise appropriate techniques to select the "best" execution plan. This requires first to define a cost model to compare service execution plans solving the same query. Then we need to build search strategies based on this cost model.

4.2.1 QoWS-aware Cost Model

We propose a cost model based mainly on the concept of *QoWS* as introduced earlier. The general idea is to define what constitutes an "optimal" service execution plan based on *QoWS* [74]. A service execution plan is built by first mapping relations to virtual operations, then locating actual Web services with concrete operations that can be matched to those virtual operations, and finally combining the different operation invocations in a way that answer the query. The first step is straightforward and does not involve any optimization decision. However, the two last steps are key in producing an optimal plan.

On the other hand, users may have preferences over how their queries are answered. They may specify as part of a query which *QoWS* parameters are important for them and how important they are. This can be done by assigning *weights*, ranging from 0 to 1, to each *QoWS* parameter. Obviously, the query infrastructure should consider default values for these weights if a user does not specify them.

Aggregating QoWS for a Service Execution Plan

One approach to rank service execution plans based on *QoWS* of individual Web services is to aggregate all its *QoWS* parameters in one single formula. An interesting method is the *Simple Additive Weighting* [97] widely used in decision making. Its ranking results are usually very close to results of more sophisticated methods [68]. This method comprises three basic steps applied to the *QoWS* of each potential plan: (i) scale the different parameters (*QoWS*) to make them comparable, (ii) apply user-supplied weights for each parameter, and (iii) finally sum up the weighted and scaled *QoWS* parameters. Service execution plans are then ranked based on the scores they obtain in the last step.

The cost model use scores obtained by the simple additive weighting method. Thus, the *objective function*, F, is defined for each service execution plan *SEP* as follows:

$$F_{saw}(SEP) = (\sum_{Q_i \in neg} \frac{Q_i^{max} - Q_i}{Q_i^{max} - Q_i^{min}} + \sum_{Q_i \in pos} \frac{Q_i - Q_i^{min}}{Q_i^{max} - Q_i^{min}})$$

Where Q_i^{max} is the maximum value for the ith *QoWS* parameter for all potential service execution plans and Q_i^{min} is the minimum.

Matching Degrees

Virtual operations are matched to concrete ones using one of the different matching that we have defined in Chapter 3. As each level delivers a different matching "precision", we assign a *matching degree* to each level to quantify this precision. We define four matching degrees for the four levels respectively: 1, $9/10$, $8/10$, and $7/10$. These values are arbitrary. Their main goal is to distinguish the different matching levels. They may be changed depending on the intended impact of these degrees on the optimization process. We define the matching degree of a service execution plan as the average of matching degrees of all its concrete operations. Values for the different matching degrees may be application specific with respect to users' needs and the intended impact on optimization.

These matching degrees could be returned with the query results giving users some hints on how the query has been processed. It will be then up to the user to accept or reject the results. A better approach would be to send those matching degrees before invoking operations. This way the user may decide to stop the query before it starts or while in execution.

Another use of these matching degrees is to include them as part of the cost model. For example, using the object function F_{saw}, matching degrees could be introduced either directly into the formula or in the computation of the different *QoWSs* of the service execution plan. In the first case, the objective function would be

$$F_{saw\&md}(SEP) = matching\_degree(SEP)$$

$$\times \left(\sum_{Q_i \in neg} \frac{Q_i^{max} - Q_i}{Q_i^{max} - Q_i^{min}} + \sum_{Q_i \in pos} \frac{Q_i - Q_i^{min}}{Q_i^{max} - Q_i^{min}} \right)$$

In the second case, the same objective function F_{saw} is used. However, for all negative $QoWS$, the value used in computing the aggregated $QoWS(SEP)$ is replaced by $QoWS(ws_j)/matching\_degree(ws_j)$ for all Web services ws_j used in SEP. For all positive $QoWS$, the value used in computing the aggregated $QoWS(SEP)$ is replaced by $QoWS(ws_j) * matching\_degree(ws_j)$ for all Web services ws_j used in SEP. The corresponding values are either lowered or increased to reflect the effect of the matching level.

Accounting for Web Service Ratings

As part of our query approach, Web services are monitored and "rated" according to their behavior in terms of delivering the promised $QoWS$. These ratings are included in the cost model as they enable adjusting advertised $QoWS$ according to the actual behavior of Web services. Like matching degrees, they can be included in the objective function F_{saw} either directly into the formula or in the computation of the different $QoWS$ of the service execution plan. In the former case, we could approximate the rating of the service execution plan by the average of ratings of Web services used in the plan. In the latter case, $QoWS$ of individual Web services are weighted by their ratings in computing the $QoWS$ of the service execution plan using the corresponding aggregation functions. For all negative $QoWS$, the value used in computing the aggregated $QoWS(SEP)$ is replaced by $QoWS(ws_j)/rating(ws_j)$ for all Web services ws_j used in SEP. For all positive $QoWS$, the value used in computing the aggregated $QoWS(SEP)$ is replaced by $QoWS(ws_j) * rating(ws_j)$ for all Web services ws_j used in SEP. The corresponding values are either lowered or increased to reflect the effect of the ratings.

Optimization Problem Specification

Based on the previous discussion, we can now specify the targeted optimization problem (Figure 4.3). Given a query Q expressed using relations from $\mathscr{R}$, find operations from $\mathscr{S}$ that form a feasible service execution plan SEP that maximizes the objective function F:

$$F_{smr}(SEP) = \left(\sum_{Q_i \in neg} W_i \frac{Q_i^{max} - Q_i}{Q_i^{max} - Q_i^{min}} + \sum_{Q_i \in pos} W_i \frac{Q_i - Q_i^{min}}{Q_i^{max} - Q_i^{min}} \right)$$

Where neg and pos are the set of negative and positive $QoWS$ respectively. W_i are weights assigned by users to each parameter. Q_i is the value of the ith $QoWS$ of the service execution plan obtained through the aggregation functions from Table 4.1 adjusted to the ratings and matching degrees obtained by individual Web services forming the plan. Q_i^{max} is the maximum value for the ith QoWS parameter for all potential service execution plans and Q_i^{min} is the minimum. These two values can be computed by considering matching concrete operations with the highest and lowest values for the ith QoWS adjusted to ratings and matching degrees. We do not have to generate all potential execution plans. We elect to include both the ratings and the matching degrees in computing the QoWS as this will give a more accurate evaluation of the service execution plans and hence provide for a more precise comparison for optimization purpose.

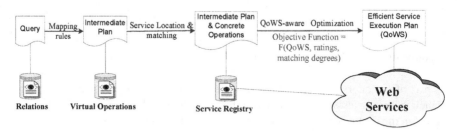

Fig. 4.3   Query Optimization Outline

4.2.2 Optimization Strategies

Without loss of generality, we assume that the query contains N virtual operations and each virtual operation could be matched to M concrete operations. In a nutshell, the optimization strategy consists of:

- Selecting for each virtual operation, a concrete operation amongst M potential concrete operations.
- Making sure that whenever a given Web service is selected using a discounted QoWS then its partner should be present in the plan.
- Ordering the concrete operations in a way that the obtained plan is feasible.

There are two straightforward solutions for our optimization problems: *exhaustive search* and *local selection*. In the exhaustive strategy, we generate all possible service execution plans and select the best one. Obviously, this strategy does not miss the optimal plan. However, this is achieved at a prohibitive cost. Indeed, assume that the query is translated to N virtual operations and that each virtual operation could be matched to as many as M concrete operations. The total number of potential service execution plans is in this case M^N. The computation cost of such an exhaustive approach would be $O(M^N)$. This is clearly not an option if we consider the ever expanding service space where a single functionality could be offered by a large number of Web services. In the local selection strategy, the best concrete operation, based on operations' *QoWS*, is selected for each virtual operation in the query. Such strategy may lead to sub-optimal solutions if some constraints need to be enforced. This is especially true for the case of *discount relationships* where we need to check that both concrete operations (in fact, their respective Web services) involved in a discount relationship are used in the selected service execution plan.

We are faced with an optimization problem for which there is a very large number of solutions (in the $O(M^N)$ order). The issue is to select the optimal or a near optimal solution in a realistic time scale. This means a time much less than that needed to examine all solutions.

In the following, we present algorithms that take into account the presence of specific constraints: binding requirements and discount relationships. These algorithms have been designed in a way to find a balance between finding the optimal plan and processing a query in an acceptable time. For comparison purpose, we start by outlining an algorithm based on an exhaustive strategy that can support any type of constraints. This algorithm serves as a reference to check how far any other algorithm is missing the optimal plan. This is important for experimenting our different algorithms.

4.2.3 Exhaustive Algorithm

For experimental purposes, we consider the case of an optimization algorithm based on exhaustive search. All other algorithms will be compared to it to check whether they miss the optimal plan and how far they miss it. The exhaustive algorithm starts by searching all potential concrete operations that match each virtual operation in the query. It then computes the *QoWS* of all possible service execution plans based on the located concrete operations taking into account all *discount relationships* among the corresponding Web services. Taking into account discount relationships increases the number of potential service execution plans since the same Web services may be used with different *QoWS*.

Exhaustive Algorithm
Input: Conjunctive query $Q(X) : - R_1(X_1), R_2(X_2), ..., R_n(X_n), C_1, C_2, ..., C_m$
Output: Feasible and optimal service execution plan.
    • **Initialization**
1:     For each R_i in Q
2:        $V = V \cup \{Vop \:/\: Vop$ is obtained from the mapping rule of $R_i\}$
3:     EndFor
    • **Computation of all Potential Service Execution Plans**
4:     For All $Vop_i \in V$
         /* Get all concrete operations matching Vop_i */
5:        $ConcOpSet[i]$ = lookupAllOperations(Vop_i)
6:        If $ConcOpSet[i] = Null$ Then
7:            return ($\emptyset$) /* The query is not answerable */
8:        EndIf
9:     EndFor
10:   bestPlan = $\emptyset$

11:     $F_{bestPlan} = 0$ /* Initial value for the objective function */
12:     $potentialPlan = bestPlan$
13:     While $morePotentialPlan$ /* Loop while there are still plans to generate */
            /* Get the next potential plan */
14:         $potentialPlan$ = getNextPlan($V, ConcOpSet, nextPlan$)
            /* If the current potential plan is feasible and has a better quality, */
            /* replace the current best plan */
15:         If feasible($potentialPlan$) and $F_{smr}(potentialPlan) > F_{smr}(bestPlan)$ Then
16:             $bestPlan = nextPlan$
17:             $F_{smr}(bestPlan) = F_{smr}(nextPlan)$
18:         EndIf
19:     EndWhile
     • **End** /* Build execution graph, if any, based on binding requirements */
20:     IF $bestPlan = \emptyset$ Then
21:         return($\emptyset$)
22:     Else
23:         return(buildDG($bestPlan$))

The *Exhaustive Algorithm* consists of three main phases. In the first phase (1–3), the set of virtual operations is obtained through mapping rules of relations appearing in the query. In fact, all algorithms will need to go through this initialization phase. In the second phase (4–19), all potential service execution plans are generated and compared based on the objective function F_{smr} that we have defined. A service execution plan with the greater value for this function than the current best plan is selected if it is feasible (18). The third phase (20–23) builds the execution graph for the best service execution plan if one is found. If the query is not answerable an empty set is returned.

4.2.4 Optimal Service Execution Plan in Presence of Binding Requirements

In the following, we present two algorithms to process queries over Web services that focus on respecting the binding requirements of the different operations. Both algorithms sequence operation invocations based on binding requirements and use local selection optimization [74]. The "best" concrete operation based on *QoWS* is selected for each virtual operation using the same simple additive method described in Section 4.2.1 for service execution plans taking into account matching degrees and ratings. We call the first algorithm *Simple-Sequencing* and the second *DG-Algorithm* (*DG* refers to the dependency graph being used). The major differences between the two algorithms are: The *Simple-Sequencing* algorithm may invoke the lookup function several times until getting the best concrete operation that does not violate any binding requirement. *DG-Algorithm* uses dependencies on virtual operations to request only concrete operations with the exact required binding requirements (input and output). Both algorithms base their optimization on individually selecting the best match (concrete operation) for each virtual operation appearing in the query and do not take into account discount relationships.

Simple-Sequencing Algorithm

Simple-Sequencing Algorithm
Input: Conjunctive query $Q(X)$ $: - R_1(X_1), R_2(X_2), ..., R_n(X_n), C_1, C_2, ..., C_m$
Output: Feasible and efficient service execution plan S.
- **Initialization**
1:     *Bindings* = Set of bound variables /* Initially bound variables as specified in the query */
2:     $V = \emptyset$ /* Virtual operations, initially empty */
3:     $S = \emptyset$ /* Sequence of sets of operations. Operations in the same set */
       /* can be invoked concurrently since there is no binding requirement amongst them*/
4:     For each R_i in Q /* Query Unfolding*/
5:         $V = V \cup \{Vop \,/\, Vop$ is obtained from the mapping rule of $R_i\}$
6:     EndFor
- **Virtual Operations Ordering**
7:     $nseq = 0$ /* Number of sets in S */
8:     While $V \neq \emptyset$
9:         $Seq = \emptyset$
10:        For $Vop \in V$
11:            If $In(Vop) \in Bindings$ Then
12:                $Seq = Seq \cup Vop$
13:        EndFor
14:        If $Seq = \emptyset$ Then
15:            return $(\emptyset)$ /* The query is not answerable */
16:        $V = V - Seq$
17:        $S = S + Seq$
18:        $nseq$++
19:        $Bindings = Bindings \cup \{x/\, x \in Out(Vop) \wedge Vop \in Seq\}$
20:    EndWhile
- **Service Discovery & Operations Matching**
21:    For $i = 0, i < nseq$
22:        $ExcludedOp = \emptyset$
23:        For $Vop \in Seq_i$
24:            **lookup**: $ConcOp$ = lookupBestOperation($Vop, ExcludedOp$)
25:            If $ConcOp = Null$ Then
26:                return $(\emptyset)$ /* The query is not answerable */
27:            If $Out(ConcOp) < Out(Vop)$ Then
28:                If $\exists Seq_{i+k}(k > 0), (In(Vop) - In(ConcOp)) \subseteq In(Seq_{i+k})$ and
                   $\forall Seq_{i+l}(0 < l < k), \neg((In(Vop) - In(ConcOp)) \subset Seq_{i+l})$ Then
29:                    Goto **lookup** /* Get another ConcOp since it has jeopardized */
                       /* the invocation of subsequent operations */
30:            Replace Vop by $ConcOp$ in Seq_i
31:        EndFor
32:    EndFor
- **Build execution graph using the sequence S and Binding requirements**
33:    return(buildDG(S))

The *Simple-Sequencing Algorithm* consists of four phases. The first phase (1–6) is self explanatory. The set S would contain the result of the algorithm. In (4–6), the set of virtual operations is obtained through mapping rules of relations appearing in the query. In the second phase (7–20), virtual operations are selected if they can be invoked using available bindings (11). If there is no operation that can be invoked (14), the query is not answerable. Selected virtual operations are then added to S (19) and available bindings are updated (17). In the third phase (21–32), virtual operations are replaced by concrete operations while making sure that the obtained sequence is still feasible using available bindings. If the function *lookupBestOperation* cannot find a match for a given virtual operation (25), the query is not answerable (26). If the function returns a partial match where the concrete operation returns fewer output variables (27), the algorithm checks that there is no virtual operation in the sequence whose inputs depend from the missing outputs (28). Otherwise (29), the lookup function is called again to find a different match. Finally (30), the virtual operation in S is replaced by its corresponding concrete operation. The fourth phase (7–20) builds the execution graph based on S.

The *lookupBestOperation* function returns a concrete operation with the highest value for the objective function applied to individual operation. It starts by looking for relevant Web services through available service registries using the *Category* and *Function* attributes of the virtual operation. For each returned Web service, its description is searched for operations that match the virtual operation using the different levels previously defined. The function then selects the operation with the highest value for the objective function and that does not belong to the second argument.

Dependency Graph based Algorithm

DG-Algorithm
Input: Conjunctive query $Q(X) : - R_1(X_1), R_2(X_2), ..., R_n(X_n), C_1, C_2, ..., C_m$
Output: Feasible and efficient service execution plan DG.
- **Initialization**
1:      $V = \emptyset$ /* Virtual operations, initially empty */
- **Query Unfolding**
2:      For each R_i in Q
3:          $V = V \cup \{Vop$ / Vop is obtained from the mapping rule of $R_i\}$
4:      EndFor
5:      DG = buildDG(V) /* Dependency Graph Building*/
- **Binding Requirements Determination and Operation Lookup**
6:      For $i = 0$ to $max_order(DG(V))$
7:          $C_{set} = \emptyset$ /* C_{set} is a set of concrete operations that can be invoked concurrently */
8:          For all Vop st $order(Vop) = i$
                    /* The corresponding concrete operation $ConcOp$ would not require
                       the missing input variables $missing\_input$ */
9:              If Vop has a dependency with Op_0
10:                 $missing\_input = label(Op_0, Vop)$
11:             Else
12:                 $missing\_input = \emptyset$
                    /* ConcOp should provide for output that are required by its subsequent
                       neighbors */
13:             $required\_output = \bigcup_{Vop' \text{ is a subsequent neighbor of } Vop \text{ in } DG} label(Vop, Vop')$

```
                    /* Locate the best concrete operation ConcOp that matches Vop,
                       does not require the missing input, and provide the required output */
14:                  ConcOp = lookupBestExactOperation(Vop, missing_input, required_output)
15:                  If ConcOp is found
16:                      Replace Vop by ConcOp in DG and update DG subsequently
17:                  Else
18:                      return ∅ /* Q is not answerable */
19:              EndFor
20:         EndFor
      • End
21:         Return DG
```

The *DG-Algorithm* consists of three phases. The first phase (1-5) is self explanatory. The set *S* would contain the result of the algorithm. In (2-5), the set of virtual operations is obtained through mapping rules of relations appearing in the query. The last step of this phase builds the dependency graph *DG* for virtual operations based on available bindings (see definition 4.3). In the second phase (6-20), the dependency graph is traversed following ascending order of its nodes (from 0 to the maximum order of the graph). For each virtual operation (9-12), we determine what are its input requirements that are not obtainable from any other node (*missing_input*) and the output requirements (*required_output*) that are required by all its subsequent neighbors in the graph. The *lookupBestExactOperation* function is then invoked (14) to return the "best" concrete operation that matches the virtual operation, does not require *missing_input*, and provide *required_input*. If there is no match (18), the query is not answerable. Otherwise (16) the located concrete operation is inserted in the current set (C_{set}) of operations that can be invoked concurrently. Finally (21), the updated dependency graph is returned.

4.2.5 Optimal Service Execution Plan in Presence of Discount Relationships

The main issue when optimizing queries in the presence of discount relationships is to make sure that both partners are present in the plan. This means that whenever a Web service is selected based on a discount value for one of its *QoWS*, its partner in the discount relationship should be also selected. The optimizer will be faced with several global constraints, we call it the *presence test*, to be checked against the service execution plan. For this case, we present two algorithms where one of them has two flavors. The first algorithm is based on a local bi-selection. The second algorithm iterates over an initial service execution plan by replacing one concrete operation until finding a feasible plan that satisfies the presence test or reach a threshold. The choice of the concrete operation to replace may be done using two different replacement policies.

To address the issue of binding requirements, we build the dependency graph based on virtual operations. The lookup will look only for concrete operations that satisfy input requirements as specified by the dependency graph.

Local Bi-Selection Algorithm

Local Bi-Selection Algorithm
Input: Conjunctive query $Q(X)$ $: - R_1(X_1), R_2(X_2), ..., R_n(X_n), C_1, C_2, ..., C_m$
Output: Feasible and efficient service execution plan.
  • **Initialization**
1:      $V = \emptyset$ /* Set of virtual operations */
2:      $DRCop = \emptyset$ /* Set of concrete operations selected based on discounted $QoWS$ */
            that do not have their partners in the plan */
3:      $missingPartners = \emptyset$ /* Set of missing partners */
4:      For each R_i in Q
5:          $V = V \cup \{Vop \mid Vop$ is obtained from the mapping rule of $R_i\}$
6:      EndFor
7:      $DG = \text{buildDG}(V)$
  • **Local Selection**
8:      For each $Vop \in V$
            /* Lookup the best Cop taking into account discount relationships */
9:          lookupBestDR($Vop, Cop, partner$)
10:         If $Cop = $ Null Then
11:             return($\emptyset$) /* The query is not answerable*/
12:         EndIf
13:         If $Cop \in missingPartners$ Then
14:             $missingPartners = missingPartners - Cop$
                /* Remove corresponding partners from DRCop*/
15:             $DRCop = DRCop - \{op/op$ is partner of $Cop\}$
16:         EndIf
17:         $DG = DG + Cop$ /* Update DG by replacing Vop with Cop */
18:         If $partner \neq \emptyset$ and partner $\notin DG$ Then
19:             $DRCop = DRCop + Cop$
20:             $missingPartners = missingPartners + partner$
21:         EndIf
22:     EndFor
  • **Second Local Selection**
23:     For $Cop \in DRCop$ /* Remove a Cop if partner not present */
24:         $Vop = \text{matchOf}(Cop)$ /* Get the virtual operation corresponding to Cop*/
            /* Lookup the best Cop without considering discount relationships */
25:         lookupBestNoDR(Vop, Cop')
26:         If $Cop' \in missingPartners$ Then
27:             $missingPartners = missingPartners - Cop'$
28:             remove corresponding partner(s) from $DRCop$
29:         EndIf
30:         $DG = DG - Cop + Cop'$ /* Update DG by removing Cop and replacing it by Cop' */
31:     EndFor
  • **End**
32:         return(DG)

The *Local Bi-Selection Algorithm* has also two main phases. In the first phase
(8–22), a local selection is conducted taking into account discount relationships.
Each virtual operation is replaced by the best concrete operation using the objective
function F_{smr} (applied to individual operations). Since the returned concrete operation may require the presence of a partner, we test if that partner is present. We
test also whether the located concrete operation is a partner of previous concrete

operations (13−16). In the second phase (23−31), any concrete operation missing its partners will be replaced by a concrete operation that does not require one. This operation is the next best match selected without taking into account discount relationships. Finally, the dependency graph representing the service execution plan is returned. For efficiency reasons, we assume that both functions *lookupBestDR* and *lookupBestNoDR* share common information to avoid extra computations.

Iterative Algorithm

We present now the *Iterative Algorithm* that in contrast to the *Bi-Selection Algorithm* keeps trying finding a feasible plan taking into account discount relationships.

Iterative Algorithm
Input: Conjunctive query $Q(X)$ $: − R_1(X_1), R_2(X_2), ..., R_n(X_n), C_1, C_2, ..., C_m$
Output: Feasible and efficient service execution plan S.
- **Initialization**
1:    $V = \emptyset$ /* Set of virtual operations */
2:    $C = \emptyset$ Set of matching concrete operations */
3:    $DRCop = \emptyset$ /* Set of concrete operations selected based on discounted $QoWS$ */
          that do not have their partners in the plan */
4:    $missingPartners = \emptyset$ /* Set of missing partners */
5:    For each R_i in Q
6:        $V = V \cup \{Vop \, / \, Vop$ is obtained from the mapping rule of $R_i\}$
7:    EndFor
8:    $DG = $ buildDG(V)
- **Local Selection**
9:    For each $Vop \in V$
10:       lookupBestDR$(Vop, Cop, partner)$ /* Lookup the best concrete operation */
          /* taking into account discount relationships */
11:       If $Cop = $ Null Then
12:          return$(\emptyset)$ /* The query is not answerable*/
13:       EndIf
14:       If $Cop \in missingPartners$ Then
15:          $missingPartners = missingPartners − Cop$
          /* Remove corresponding partners from $DRCop$*/
16:          $DRCop = DRCop − \{op \, / \, op \, is \, partner \, of \, Cop\}$
17:       EndIf
18:       $DG = DG + Cop$ /* Update DG by replacing Vop with Cop */
19:       If $partner \neq \emptyset$ and $partner \notin DG$Then
20:          $DRCop = DRCop + Cop$
21:          $missingPartners = missingPartners + partner$
22:       EndIf
23:    EndFor
- **Iterative Selection (first form)**
    /* Iterate until finding a feasible solution or reaching a threshold */
24:    sort$(DRCop)$ /* Sort $DRCop$ to facilitate subsequent selection of concrete operations */
24:    While $missingPartners \neq \emptyset$ and $threshold \neq 0$
          /* Remove the concrete operation that may have the less effect on $QoWS$ */
25:       $Cop = $ getBest$(DRCop)$
          /* Get the virtual operation corresponding to that concrete operation */
26:       $Vop = $ getMatch(Cop)

```
27:        lookupNextBestDR(Vop, Cop', partner) /* get the next best concrete operation */
28:        If Cop' = Null Then /* No more concrete operation to match */
29:             return(∅) /* Give up, the query may not be answerable*/
30:        EndIf
31:        If Cop ∈ missingPartners Then
32:             missingPartners = missingPartners − Cop
33:             remove corresponding partner(s) fromDRCop
34:        EndIf
35:        DG = DG − Cop + Cop' /* Update DG by removing Cop and replacing it by Cop' */
36:        If partner ≠ ∅ and partner ∉ DG Then
37:             DRCop = DRCop + Cop /* Respect the sort while updating DRCop
38:             missingPartners = missingPartners + partner
39:        EndIf
40:        threshold = threshold - 1
41:     EndFor
   • End /* Return execution graph if any*/
43:     If missingPartners = ∅ Then
44:          return((DG))
45:     Else
46:          return(∅) /* Either the query is unanswerable or the threshold has been reached */
47:     EndIf
```

After the usual initialization phase (1–8), the *Iterative Algorithm* proceeds with a local selection of the service execution plan (9–23). If the plan is not feasible with respect to discount relationships (some partners are missing), then the algorithm goes through an iterative process based on a simple heuristic (24–42). The algorithm selects the concrete operation having a missing partner that may have the least effect on *QoWS* (25). It then replaces it by its next best match. This process is repeated until a feasible plan is found or a threshold is reached. The threshold could be set in a way that the total computation time is still acceptable by users. For efficiency reasons, we assume that both functions *lookupBestDR* and *lookupNextBestDR* have shared common information to avoid extra computation.

Below is a small modification to the iteration phase of the previous algorithm. Instead of replacing only one concrete operation from *DRCop*, all concrete operations in that set are replaced.

• **Iterative Selection (second form)**
    /* Iteration until finding a feasible solution or reaching a threshold
    based on a different replacement policy */

```
24:     While missingPartners ≠ ∅ and threshold ≠ 0
25:        For all Cop ∈ DRCop
             /* Get the virtual operation corresponding to that concrete operation */
26:             Vop = getMatch(Cop)
27:             lookupNextBestDR(Vop, Cop', partner) /* Get the next best concrete
                 operations */
28:             DG = DG − Cop + Cop' /* Update DG by removing Cop and replacing it by
                 Cop' */
29:             If Cop' ∈ missingPartners Then
30:                  missingPartners = missingPartners − Cop'
31:                  remove corresponding partner(s) from DRCop
32:             EndIf
33:             If partner(Cop') ≠ ∅ and partner ∉ C Then
34:                  DRCop = DRCop + Cop
```

```
35:                missingPartners = missingPartners + partner(Cop')
36:            EndIf
37:        EndFor
38:    EndWhile
```

Simulated Annealing based Algorithm

Simulated annealing [1] is an optimization method based on a correspondence be-tween complex optimization problems and statistical mechanics. The underlying idea is the controlled introduction of perturbation in updating the solution to avoid trapping in local, but not global, optimum. The perturbation is reduced as the op-timality of the solution improves such that, at the global optimum, determinism is recovered and the solution remains optimal. Simulated annealing relies on a scheme of acceptance or rejection of a small change to the state of the system, known as the Metropolis algorithm, such that downhill moves occur with probability unity but uphill moves with probability proportional to the difference in Boltzmann weights.

We present now a simulated annealing based algorithm to optimize queries over Web services. The initial solution is obtained through local selection without consid-ering discount relationships and making sure that binding requirements are satisfied. The current solution (starting from the initial one) is perturbed by changing concrete operation(s) for one or several virtual operations. The new service execution plan is tested for feasibility in terms of binding requirements and discount relationships. Only feasible plans are considered. The objective function is computed for the new plan. It is compared to the current one. The current execution plan is replaced by the new one if it leads to a better solution otherwise the replacement takes place with a probability $\exp^{(F(SEP_1)-F(SEP_2))/T}$ as defined in the original simulated annealing algorithm.

Simulated Annealing Algorithm
Input: Conjunctive query $Q(X) : - R_1(X_1), R_2(X_2), ..., R_n(X_n), C_1, C_2, ..., C_m$
Output: Feasible and efficient service execution plan S.
- **Initialization**
```
1:      V = ∅ /* Set of virtual operations */
2:      For each R_i in Q
3:          V = V∪ {Vop / Vop is obtained from the mapping rule of R_i}
4:      EndFor
5:      DG = buildDG(V)
```
- **Local Selection**
```
6:      For each Vop ∈ V
7:          lookupBestExactNoDR(Vop, Cop) /* Lookup the best concrete operation without */
                                          /* taking into account discount relationships and requiring exact match */
8:          DG_0 = DG_0 + Cop
9:      EndFor
```
- **Annealing Iterations**
```
10:     T = T_0
11:     While (T > T_f)
12:         For max_iteration
13:             DG_1 = Perturb(DG_0)
```

```
14:         If ($F_{smr}(DG_1) > F_{smr}(DG_0)$) or $\exp^{(F(DG_1)-F(DG_0))/T}$ > random(0,1) Then
15:             $DG_0 = DG_1$
16:         EndIf
17:     EndFor
18:     $T_0 = T_0 * \alpha$
19: EndWhile
  • End
20:     return($DG_0$)
```

The *Simulated Annealing Algorithm* has three main phases. After the usual initialization phase (1–5), an initial feasible solution (6–9) is built using local selection and ignoring discount relationships. In the third phase, the algorithm continuously iterates (10–19) by perturbing the initial solution until reaching the final temperature T_f. The algorithm is guaranteed to stop since the current temperature T is decreased by a cooling rate $\alpha < 1$.

There are many parameters that need to be determined for the algorithm. These include the *initial temperature* T_0, the *final temperature* T_f, the number of iterations *max_iteration*, the *cooling rate alpha*, and the perturbation function. For the perturbation of the current solution, we need to identify the most appropriate way to modify the solution while making sure that it is still feasible (discount relationships and binding requirements). The feasibility check may require looking at more than one potential service execution plan. For the kind of perturbation to be applied, we need to characterize the neighborhood structure for a a given execution plan. This can be done, for example, by selecting a random number of virtual operations for which we seek another matching concrete operation. We have two options to decide which concrete operation to take: (i) randomly pick up a concrete operation from all potential matches for a given Vop, or (ii) get the next best Cop.

4.2.6 Compensate/Undo and Re-Optimize Approach for Supporting Postconditions

Some conditions expressed in the query can only be checked after the Web service is actually invoked. The non satisfaction of such conditions do not necessarily mean that they cannot be satisfied in all cases. Indeed, Web services offering similar functionalities may have different outcomes for such conditions. For example, in the case of the different transportation choices in the senior citizen scenario depicted in Figure 1.4. The different prices and pricing modes may not be obtainable up-front from the different Web services but are only available once actual operations are invoked. Thus, the optimizer should provide for mechanisms to check those conditions at runtime and eventually replace the Web service(s) that may have caused the non satisfaction of the conditions. This should be done while ensuring optimization.

We propose a technique based on *compensate/undo* and *re-optimize*. The idea is that the query is first optimized using one of the above algorithms. At *runtime*, if a post-condition fails, we need to determine which operations to undo or re-optimize.

A simple solution would be to select all the operations providing output used in that condition. If this is not possible then the query is stopped and the user is informed. Otherwise, the execution is suspended and the remaining part of the service execution plan is re-optimized using the same algorithm as initially. The execution is resumed after the re-optimization step. Note that if more than one operation is involved, it may be possible to select only some of them to get the failed condition satisfied by using new operations.

Table 4.1 Quality of Web Service for a Service Execution Plan

QoWS parameter	Aggregation function
Latency	$$\sum_{ws_i \in max} latency(ws_i)$$
Availability	$$\prod_{i=1}^{N} av(ws_i)$$
Accessibility	$$\prod_{i=1}^{N} acc(ws_i)$$
Encryption	$$\frac{1}{N}\sum_{i=1}^{N} enc(ws_i) \ or \ \prod_{i=1}^{N} enc(ws_i)$$
Authentication	$$\frac{1}{N}\sum_{i=1}^{N} aut(ws_i) \ or \ \prod_{i=1}^{N} aut(ws_i)$$
Access control	$$\frac{1}{N}\sum_{i=1}^{N} act(ws_i) \ or \ \prod_{i=1}^{N} act(ws_i)$$
Privacy policy	$$\frac{1}{N}\sum_{i=1}^{N} pp(ws_i) \ or \ \prod_{i=1}^{N} pp(ws_i)$$
Information sharing	$$\frac{1}{N}\sum_{i=1}^{N} is(ws_i) \ or \ \prod_{i=1}^{N} is(ws_i)$$
Information disclosure	$$\frac{1}{N}\sum_{i=1}^{N} id(ws_i) \ or \ \prod_{i=1}^{N} id(ws_i)$$
Usage fee	$$\sum_{i=1}^{N} fee(ws_i)$$
Reputation	$$\frac{1}{N}\sum_{i=1}^{N} rep(ws_i)$$

Chapter 5
Implementation and Experiments

Abstract In this chapter, we report on the implementation and experiments for our query infrastructure over Web services. The implementation is conducted in the context of WebDG, a digital government prototype that provides access to e-government databases and services related to social services. As a prototype, WebDG supports access to only few e-government services. Thus, it cannot represent the large number of Web services available on the Web. It is then necessary to asses our approach through experiments on synthetic data. The goal of these experiments is to measure the cost of the different algorithms and the quality of the service execution plans they generate. We focus on computing the time it takes each algorithm to reach a decision. The quality of their results is simply the objective function, F_{smr}, as defined for a service execution plan in the previous chapter. These different results are then compared together under different scenarios and constraints.

5.1 WebDG – A Web Service based Infrastructure for Digital Government

WebDG is the result of a joint project involving Virginia Tech, Purdue University, the *Indiana*'s *Family and Social Services Administration* (FSSA), and the Department for the Aging. FSSA provides welfare programs to assist low income citizens, strengthen families and children, and help elderly and disabled people. The Department for the Aging focuses on senior citizens seeking support and social benefits. The process of collecting social benefits within both agencies is currently time-consuming and frustrating. Citizens must often visit different offices located within and outside their hometown. Case officers need to delve into a myriad of applications depending on specific citizens' situations. For each situation, they must manually: (i) determine applications that appropriately satisfy citizens' needs, (ii) determine how to access each application, and (iii) combine the results returned by different applications. All of the above interactions must be conducted while making sure that citizens' information is not divulged to unauthorized entities. This difficulty in obtaining the much needed help hinders the ability of citizens to become self-dependent with all the consequences on their health and well-being.

To facilitate the use of welfare applications and hence expeditiously satisfy citizens' needs, we wrap these applications by *Web services*. Adopting Web services in e-government enables: (i) *standardized* description, discovery, and invocation of welfare programs, (ii) *efficient querying of Web services*, (iii) *composition* of pre-existing services to provide *value added* services, and (iv) *uniform* handling of privacy issues.

The development of techniques to efficiently access e-government services while preserving citizens' privacy is at the core of this project. In this chapter, we describe the design and implementation of an infrastructure for e-government services called *WebDG* (*Web Digital Government*) [27, 30, 61, 29, 62].

5.1.1 Organizing Web Services in WebDG

Interactions among *WebDG* services involve three types of participants: *provider*, *registry*, and *consumer*. *Providers* are bureaus/divisions within FSSA (e.g., Bureau of Family Resources), the different Area Agencies of Aging, or external agencies (e.g., US Department of Health and Human Services). They define descriptions of their services (e.g., operations, network location) and publish them in the *registry*. *Consumers* access the registry to locate services of interest. They include citizens, case officers, and other e-government services. The registry returns the description of each relevant service. Consumers use this description to "understand" how to use the corresponding Web service.

WebDG services are described in WSDL (*Web Services Description Language*), a standard for describing operational features of Web services [35]. Each operation has one of the following modes: *one-way, notification, request-response*, or *solicit-response*. In a *one-way* (*notification*) operation, the service receives (sends) a message. In a *request-response* (*solicit-response*) operation, the service receives (sends) a message and sends (receives) a correlated message. For example, WIC service offers a *request-response* operation namely, checkEligibility. This operation receives a message including citizen's income and family size. It returns another message indicating if the citizen is eligible for the WIC program. WSDL descriptions are stored using *UDDI* (*Universal Description, Discovery and Integration*), a standard for publishing and discovering Web services [92]. For example, the registration of Medicaid service includes a URL needed to communicate with this service and a pointer to its WSDL description.

Communication among *WebDG* services is enabled through SOAP (*Simple Object Access Protocol*) standard [36]. The use of XML-based messaging over well-established protocols (e.g., HTTP and SMTP) makes SOAP platform-independent. Many key industry leaders participate in the SOAP development. SOAP is still at its early stage and hence does not yet meet all scalability requirements needed for Web applications. Some scalability problems may be overcome in e-government environments. Using complex data types in SOAP requests may add an overhead for processing those requests. However, the data types used in e-government are generally agreed upon *a priori* between government agencies, hence reducing this overhead.

Composing WebDG Services

Service composers (e.g., self-sufficiency workers) provide a high level specification of the desired composition. Based on composability rules, *WebDG* generates a *composition plan*. Each *plan* gives the list of outsourced services and how they interact with each other to achieve the desired composition. Composition has been the focus of a different research [62].

Preserving Privacy

Privacy is a major issue that needs to be addressed in e-government. Citizens generally divulge sensitive information (e.g., SSN, salary) when accessing e-government services. Two characteristics add to the complexity of the privacy problem in e-government: the sharing of citizens' information amongst government agencies and the different citizens' requirements with respect to their privacy. Privacy has been the focus of a different research [80].

5.1.2 WebDG Implementation

WebDG system is implemented across a network of *Solaris* workstations. Citizens and case officers access *WebDG* via a *Graphical User Interface* (GUI) implemented using HTML/Servlet (Figure 5.1). *WebDG* currently includes seven (7) FSSA applications implemented in Java (JDK 1.3). These applications are wrapped by WSDL descriptions. We use the *Axis's Java2WSDL* utility in *IBM's Web Services Toolkit* to automatically generate WSDL descriptions from Java class files. WSDL service descriptions are published into UDDI registry. We adopt *Systinet's WASP UDDI Standard 3.1* as our UDDI toolkit. *Cloudscape* (4.0) database is used as a UDDI registry.

WebDG uses the *service management client* provided within *Apache SOAP* (2.2) to deploy e-government services. *Apache SOAP* provides not only server-side infrastructure for deploying and managing service, but also client-side API for invoking those services. Each service has a *deployment descriptor*. The descriptor includes the unique identifier of the Java class to be invoked, session scope of the class, and operations in the class available for the clients. Each service is deployed using its descriptor and the URL of the *Apache SOAP servlet rpcrouter* as input arguments.

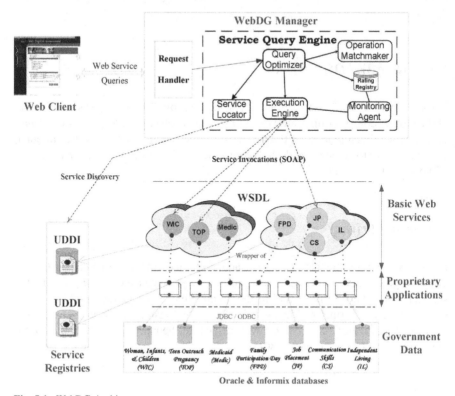

Fig. 5.1 WebDG Architecture

5.1.3 Implementation of the Query Infrastructure in WebDG

The *Service Query Engine* is responsible for the correct and optimal execution of Web service queries in WebDG. Web service queries are expressed as conjunctive queries over relations defined for social services. The Service Query Engine includes the following modules:

- *Service Locator* – The *Service Locator* discovers WSDL descriptions by accessing the UDDI registry. It implements *UDDI Inquiry Client* using WASP UDDI API.

- *Operation Matchmaker* – The Matchmaker interacts with the *Service Locator* to retrieve the services' descriptions in WSDL and determines the concrete operations to use in the service execution plan. WSDL descriptions (augmented with semantic attributes that we have defined) are parsed and concrete operations are matched to virtual operations using one of the matching modes.
- *Monitoring Agent* – This module is responsible for monitoring Web service invocations. Its goal is to assess their behavior in terms of the delivered *QoWS*. The monitoring agent maintains a local repository for ratings and other information to compute those ratings. An entry is added to this repository the first time a given Web service is being used by the query infrastructure.
- *Query Optimizer* – This is the central component of the *Query Engine*. It task is to determines the best service execution plan for a given query. It uses one of the algorithms that we presented in Section 4.2.2. It interacts with all other modules to achieve its goal.
- *Execution Engine* – After the optimizer generates an efficient service execution plan, the plan is handed over to the execution engine. The execution engine enacts the service execution plan by actually invoking Web services using SOAP. We use *SOAP Binding Stubs* which are implemented using Apache SOAP API for this purpose.

5.2 Complexity of the Proposed Algorithms

A critical goal of our query infrastructure is to get the optimal or near optimal service execution plan in terms of *QoWS* in an acceptable time. Due to the nature of the environment, the number of potential solutions that need to be checked is exponential. As a first step to assess the different algorithms that we have presented, we compute the complexity in time of each one of them. This will give us a first hand glimpse on how these different algorithms would behave in experiments or actual settings. We assume that the time to get Web services descriptions from the UDDI registry to match their concrete operations with virtual operations is a constant value.

Parameters for Complexity Computation

Given a query Q, we define several parameters for the computation time of the different algorithms. Some parameters are algorithm-specific.

- N number of virtual operations appearing in Q after query unfolding.
- M average number of concrete operations that could be matched to a given virtual operation.
- μ average number of discount relationships that a Web service is involved in.
- T_0 initial temperature for the *simulated annealing algorithm*.
- T_f final temperature for the *simulated annealing algorithm*.

- α cooling rate for the *simulated annealing algorithm*.
- I maximum iterations for the *simulated annealing algorithm*.

Exhaustive Algorithm

Time in the *exhaustive algorithm* is dominated by the iteration over all potential service execution plans. Since there are M potential concrete operations that can match any virtual operation, the algorithm needs to generate M^N different plans to find the best one. The complexity of this algorithm is in the order of $O(M^N)$.

Simple-Sequencing Algorithm

The *simple-sequence algorithm* has two main phases that takes much of the processing time. Virtual operations ordering based on binding requirements and iterative local selection of concrete operations. In the worst case, the ordering phase may find only one virtual operation that can be ordered based on available bindings at each iteration. This is approximated by a time complexity of $O(N^2)$. The iterative local selection requires to iterate over all virtual operations. For each operation, it needs to find the best concrete operation. Finding the best concrete operation requires a sort that takes $O(M \times \log M)$. The second phase is approximated by $O(N \times M \times \log M)$. Note that building the execution graph requires only N iterations in the worst case as the previous ordering phase has done most of the work by providing a sequence of set of operations. The complexity of the *simple-sequence algorithm* is in the order of $O(N^2 + N \times M \times \log M)$.

DG-Algorithm

In the *DG-algorithm*, we need first to build the dependency graph from the set of virtual operations and then get the best matching concrete operation with some restrictions on input and output. Building the dependency graph requires at most N^2 iterations. The second phase iterates over all virtual operations and requires a sort that takes $O(M \times \log M)$. The complexity of the *DG-algorithm* is in the order of $O(N^2 + N \times M \times \log M)$.

Local Bi-Selection Algorithm

The *local bi-selection algorithm* has three main phases. The first phase, building the dependency graph, requires at most N^2 iterations. The second phase looks for the best concrete operation while taking into account discount relationships for each virtual operation. This phase requires a sort that takes $O(\mu \times M \times \log(\mu \times M))$ where μ is the average number of discount relationships per operation. The third phase replaces the concrete operations that may have missing partners. In the worst case, this applies to all operations N. It also requires a $O(\mu \times M)$ scan to get the best concrete operation without discount relationships. The *local bi-selection algorithm* can be approximated by of $O(N^2 + N \times \mu \times M \times \log(\mu \times M) + N \times \mu \times M \times)$ which in facts is in the order of $O(N^2 + N \times \mu \times M \times \log(\mu \times M))$.

Iterative Algorithm

The *iterative algorithm* has three main phases. The first phase, building the dependency graph, requires at most N^2 iterations. The second phase looks for the best concrete operation while taking into account discount relationships for each virtual operation. This phase requires a sort that takes $O(\mu \times M \times \log(\mu \times M))$ where μ is the average number of discount relationships per operation. The third phase iterates until finding a solution or reaching a threshold. It is done using two different replacement policies. The first replacement policy may takes $O(\mu \times M \times \theta)$, θ being the threshold. The second one may takes $O(\mu \times M^2 \times \theta)$. The total complexity of the algorithm is either $O(N^2 + \mu \times M \times \log(\mu \times M) + \mu \times M \times \theta)$ using the first replacement policy or $O(N^2 + \mu \times M \times \log(\mu \times M) + \mu \times M^2 \times \theta)$ using the second policy.

Simulated Annealing

The two first phases, building the dependency graph and local selection, takes $O(N^2)$ and $O(N \times M \times \log M)$ respectively. The third phase depends on several parameters inherent to the annealing process. It has two nested loops, the inner loop runs for I iterations. Based on the stop condition of the outer loop $(T_0 > T_F)$ and the way that T_0 converge to T_F, the number of iterations for the outer loop is approximated by $\log(T_F/T_0)/\log \alpha$. We assume that the perturbation function has a constant value for its running time. Thus, the total complexity for this algorithm is $O(N^2 + M \times \log M + I \times \log(T_F/T_0)/\log \alpha)$.

Table 5.1 summarizes the complexities in time of the different algorithms.

Table 5.1 QoWS for a Service Execution Plan

Algorithm	Complexity
Exhaustive	$O(M^N)$
Simple-Sequencing	$O(N^2 + N \times M \times \log M)$
DG	$O(N^2 + N \times M \times \log M)$
Local Bi-Selection	$O(N^2 + \mu \times M \times \log(\mu \times M) + N \times M \times \log M)$
Iterative (first form)	$O(N^2 + \mu \times M \times \log(\mu \times M) + \mu \times M \times \theta)$
Iterative (second form)	$O(N^2 + \mu \times M \times \log(\mu \times M) + \mu \times M^2 \times \theta)$
Simulated Annealing	$O(N^2 + M \times \log M + I \times \log(T_F/T_0)/\log \alpha)$

5.3 Analytical Evaluation

In this section, we look at the processing time in more details. This will give us an idea on the type of results that we should expect from the experiments. The processing time varies from on algorithm to another and depends on several variables and parameters. Some of the variables and parameters are specific to the algorithm.

5.3.1 Bi-Selection Algorithm

Let us compute the processing time of the *bi-selection algorithm.* The basic formula for this is:

$$Time_{bi-selec} = Time_{DG} + Time_{localSelec} + Time_{secondSelec}$$

Without loss of generality, we need to make some assumptions to be able to detail the above formula. We consider the following parameters: μ_{DG} is the average number of operations that can be run in parallel. It corresponds to the number of nodes having the same order in the dependency graph. P_{DR} is the probability that a Web service is involved in a discount relationship. $P_{firstTime}$ is the probability that a concrete operation selected in the first phase of the algorithm has its partner in the service execution plan. We assume that $time_{lookup}$, the time to lookup for concrete operations from the service registry, is a constant.

Building the dependency graph requires at each order i of the graph to check if the $(N - i \times \mu_{DG})$ remaining operations have a dependency with operations in the previous order. Thus,

$$Time_{DG} = N + \sum_{j=1}^{N/\mu_{DG}} \mu_{DG} \times (N - j \times \mu_{DG})$$

which is transformed into:

$$Time_{DG} = \frac{N^2 + (2 + \mu_{DG}) \times N}{2}$$

The local selection consists mainly on matching the N virtual operations to the best concrete operations amongst M possibilities while taking into account discount relationships. The time depends mainly on the lookup in the service registry and sorting Web services based on *QoWS*. Thus,

$$Time_{localSelec} = N \times (time_{lookup} + ((1 - P_{DR}) + P_{DR} \times \mu \times M) \times \log((1 - P_{DR})$$
$$+ P_{DR} \times \mu \times M))$$

We should note that only the concrete operations that are likely to be subject to discount relationships have been multiplied by μ, the average number of discount relationships per concrete operation. The cost of the second selection is a simple scan to find the next best concrete operation without discount relationships for all operations that have missed it in the first phase. We assume that the scan gets the first operation with no discount relationships at half way of the total number of operations with discount relationships $((P_{DR} \times \mu \times M)/2)$.

$$Time_{secondSelec} = (1 - P_{firstTime}) \times N \times P_{DR} \times \mu \times M/2$$

Finally, the total time for the algorithm:

$$
\begin{aligned}
Time_{bi-selec} = & \frac{N^2 + (2 + \mu_{DG}) \times N}{2} \\
& + N \times (time_{lookup} + ((1 - P_{DR}) + P_{DR} \times \mu \times M) \times log((1 - P_{DR}) \\
& + P_{DR} \times \mu \times M)) \\
& + (1 - P_{firstTime}) \times N \times P_{DR} \times \mu \times M/2
\end{aligned}
$$

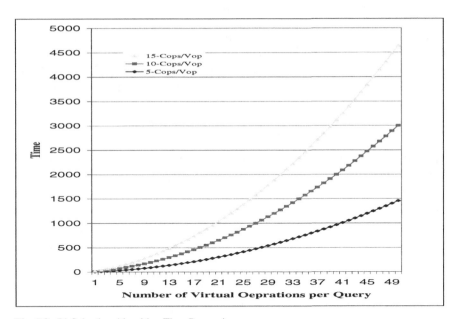

Fig. 5.2 Bi-Selection Algorithm Time Processing

Figure 5.2 shows the running time of the *bi-selection algorithm* by varying the size of the query (average number of virtual operations N) for different values of M (the number of potential concrete operations); 5, 10, and 15 respectively. We assume the following values for the different parameters. $P_{DR} = 0.3; P_{firstTime} = 0.5; \mu = 1; \mu_{DG} = 2; time_{lookup} = 1$. We notice that after around 20 virtual operations per query, the processing time grows rapidly. Having more concrete operations to match always increases the processing time.

5.3.2 Iterative Algorithm

The basic formula for the *iterative algorithm* is similar to the *bi-selection algorithm*:

$$Time_{iterative} = Time_{DG} + Time_{localSelec} + Time_{iterativeSelec}$$

The two first components of the processing time are computed in the same way. Thus, we have:

$$Time_{DG} = \frac{N^2 + (2 + \mu_{DG}) \times N}{2}$$

and

$$Time_{localSelec} = N \times (time_{lookup} + ((1 - P_{DR}) + P_{DR} \times \mu \times M) \times log((1 - P_{DR}) + P_{DR} \times \mu \times M)$$

For the third component, we have two replacement policies. We assume that the algorithm reaches a decision before the threshold. For this purpose, we make the simple assumption that the set of missing partners decreases with a certain constant probability $P_{decrease}$. The set of missing partners geometrically decreases at each iteration with a rate defined by $P_{decrease}$. If we assume that in the last iteration, we have only 1 missing partner, after k iterations $P_{decrease}^k \times N_0 = 1$, where N_0 is the initial size of the missing partners set. We approximate N_0 by $P_{decrease} \times N$. Hence: $k = (\log 1 - \log(P_{decrease} \times N))/ \log P_{decrease}$. Thus, the time for the first replacement policy is:

$$Time_{iterativeSelec1} = -\log(P_{decrease} \times N)/\log P_{decrease} * (Time_{getBest} + Time_{insertDRCop})$$

$Time_{getBest}$ is a constant and $Time_{insertDRCop}$ is the time of a search in a sorted structure ($DRCop$). Thus,

$$
\begin{aligned}
Time_{iterative1} = {} & \frac{N^2 + (2 + \mu_{DG}) \times N}{2} \\
& + N * (time_{lookup} + ((1 - P_{DR}) + P_{DR} \times \mu \times M)log((1 - P_{DR}) + P_{DR} \times \mu \times M) \\
& + (-\log P_{decrease} N/\log P_{decrease})(1 + \log(-\log(P_{decrease}\ timesN)/\log P_{decrease}))
\end{aligned}
$$

For the second replacement policy, all concrete operations are replaced.

$$Time_{iterativeSelec2} = (\log(P_{decrease} \times N)/\log P_{decrease})^2$$

Thus,

$$
\begin{aligned}
Time_{iterative1} = {} & \frac{N^2 + (2 + \mu_{DG}) \times N}{2} \\
& + N \times (time_{lookup} + ((1 - P_{DR}) + P_{DR} \times \mu \times M)log((1 - P_{DR}) + P_{DR} \times \mu \times M) \\
& + (\log(P_{decrease} \times N)/\log P_{decrease})^2
\end{aligned}
$$

We assume the following values for the different other parameters. $P_{DR} = 0.3; P_{firstTime} = 0.5; \mu = 1; \mu_{DG} = 2; time_{lookup} = 1; P_{decrease} = 0.98$. Figures 5.3 and 5.4 show the running time of the *iterative algorithm* (with the first and second replacement policy respectively) by varying the size of the query (average number of virtual operations N) for different values of M; 5, 10, and 15 respectively. In the second replacement policy, processing time increases much rapidly than in the first. This is due to the extra iterations being done in the second case.

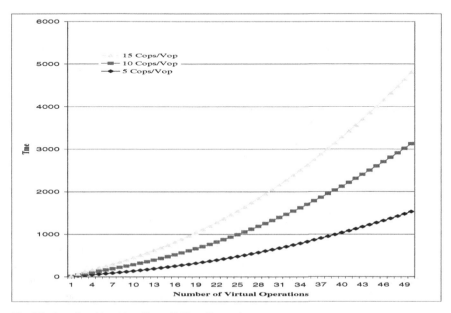

Fig. 5.3 Iterative Algorithm (form 1) Time Processing

5.3.3 Simulated Annealing Algorithm

The basis formula for the *simulated annealing algorithm* is similar to the *bi-selection algorithm*:

$$Time_{annealing} = Time_{DG} + Time_{localSelec} + Time_{annealingIterations}$$

The time to build the dependency graph is the same. Thus, we have:

$$Time_{DG} = \frac{N^2 + (2 + \mu_{DG}) \times N}{2}$$

The time of the local selection is a bit different as we do not take into account discount relationships. Thus,

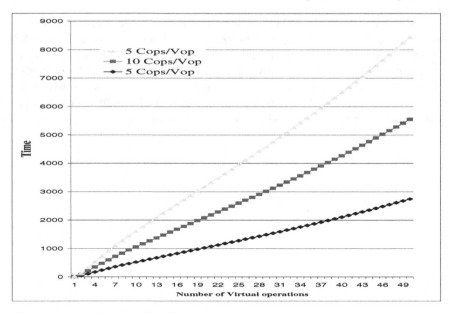

Fig. 5.4 Iterative Algorithm (form 2) Time Processing

$$Time_{localSelec} = N \times M \times \log M$$

The third component depends on the different annealing parameters, the overall number of iterations is approximated by $I \times \log(T_f/T_0)/\log\alpha$. At each iteration, the current plan is perturbed and its objective function is computed. We assume a constant value for the perturbation function and we approximate the objective function by N. Thus,

$$Time_{annealing} = \frac{N^2 + (2 + \mu_{DG}) \times N}{2} + N \times M \times \log M$$
$$+ I \times \log((T_f/T_0)/\log\alpha) \times (1 + N)$$

Figure 5.5 shows the running time of the *simulated annealing algorithm* by varying the size of the query (average number of virtual operations N) for different values of M; 5, 10, and 15 respectively. We assume the following values for the different other parameters. $time_{lookup} = 1; I = 1000; T_f = 1; T_o = 100; \alpha = 0.97$. The simulated annealing shows a dramatic increase compared to the previous algorithms.

5.4 Experiments

The different algorithms are run under different scenarios and their results are compared. As most of our algorithms are based on heuristics, we are interested in

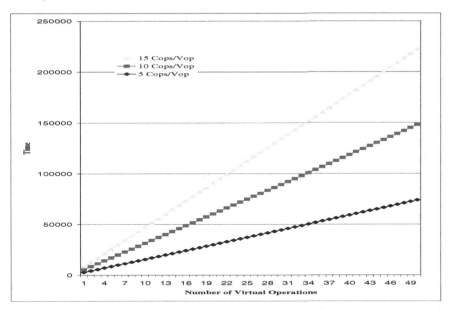

Fig. 5.5 Simulated Annealing Algorithm Time Processing

determining their failure rate in terms of finding the optimal service execution plan and how far they miss this plan. We are also interested to correlate those two information with the time spent in processing queries. Getting a "good" solution in a short period of time may be more interesting than spending much more time to get a better solution.

5.4.1 Experimental Setup

We conduct our experiments following two different approaches. The two approaches differ in the way that concrete operations are generated. In the first approach, we assume that virtual operations have been already matched to some concrete operations. In the second approach, concrete operations are obtained from randomly generated WSDL files advertised in a UDDI registry. For all of our experiments, we assume that queries are already expressed in terms of virtual operations.

First Approach

Given a virtual operation, we assume that it is already matched (using eventually different matching levels) to a given set of concrete operations. We focus then on generating *QoWS* values for these concrete operations (or their Web services). We do not consider any binding constraints. The service execution plan is necessarily feasible if conditions on discount relationships are satisfied. The general form of the experiments is:

- Queries are varied by the number of virtual operations.
- For each query, we consider different situations by varying the number of potential concrete operations per virtual operations.
- Randomly generate values of $QoWS$ parameters for the different concrete operations.
- Randomly generate discount relationships number of concrete operations involved in partnerships, $QoWS$ subject to discount, and the values of the discounts.
- Process the query using the different algorithms.
- Collect the values of the objective function obtained by the service execution plan and the time it takes for the algorithm to compute it.

We used the following settings. The number of virtual operations per query is varied from 2 to 30. The number of matching concrete operations per virtual operation varies between 0 and 30. $QoWS$ are generated in their respective domains (scalar, [0, 1], or {0, 1}). The number of concrete operations involved in discount relationships is varied between 0 and 1/3 of the available concrete operations. Without loss of generality, we assume that a Web service is involved in at most one discount relationship.

Each algorithm is run on the same generated sample of data. This would allow to compare them. The exhaustive algorithm may not be run for all cases as the size of the sample grows (in particular the number of virtual and concrete operations). For each run, we collect the values of the objective function and the processing time.

Second Approach

In the second approach, we get concrete operations from actual WSDL descriptions generated randomly based on user provided parameters (e.g., number of operations). This experiments reflect more the reality as we manipulate actual WSDL descriptions but synthetic data. This means, in particular, that some queries may not be answerable because there is no matching concrete operations for their virtual operations. This means also that the number of potential concrete operations is not the same for all virtual operations in a query. Finally, binding requirements need to be checked to make sure that a service execution plan is feasible. Figure 5.6 represents the major components of our test bed.

The experiments will be conducted similarly to the previous approach with the following differences:

- Generate WSDL descriptions by varying the number of operations and the number of Web services being generated.
- Generate virtual operations following similar principles to those used to generate the WSDL descriptions. This means in particular that the two generations, of

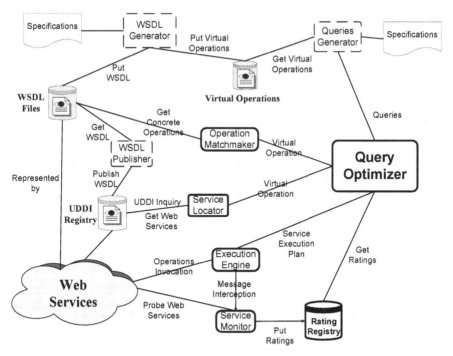

Fig. 5.6 Experimental Setup Framework

WSDL descriptions and virtual operations, will (randomly) draw their parameters from the same pool of potential operations, input and output parameters, and categories. This will be explained in more details later in this section.

- Build queries by varying the number of virtual operations that are randomly selected from the set of virtual operations generated from the previous step.
- Process the query using the different algorithms. Here we need to make sure that the obtained service execution plan is feasible both in terms of bindings requests and discount relationships constraints.
- Collect the quality score of the service execution plan and the time it takes for the algorithm to compute it. We also collect the number of potential concrete operations per virtual operations.

We use settings similar to the previous approach with few differences. The number of virtual operations per query varies from 2 to 30. The number of matching concrete operations per virtual operation depends on what is available from the generated WSDL files. $QoWS$ are generated in their respective domains (scalar, $[0, 1]$, or $\{0, 1\}$). The number of concrete operations involved in discount relationships is varied between 0 and $1/3$ of the available concrete operations. Without loss of generality, we assume that a Web service is involved in at most

Each algorithm is run on the same generated sample of data. This would allow to compare them. The exhaustive algorithm may not be run for all cases as the size of the sample grows (in particular the number of virtual and concrete operations). For each run, we collect the values of the objective function and the processing time. In addition to the total processing time, we collect the time spent in each of the *operation matchmaker* and *service locator* modules.

5.4.2 Experimental Results

In this section, we present the results that we have obtained from the different experiments. Table 5.2 gives the values of the different parameters used to generate the sample service space from our three-level query model perspective.

Table 5.2 Experimental Parameters

Parameter	Value	Notes
maxNbrVops	100	Maximum number of virtual operations
maxNbrCops	3500	Maximum number of concrete operations
maxNbrDiscountOperations	500	Maximum number of operations in a discount relationship
maxNbrInputAttributes	10	Maximum number of input attributes per operation
maxNbrOutputAttributes	10	Maximum number of output attributes per operation
maxNbrCategoryAttributes	10	Maximum number of Categories per operation
maxNbrFunctionAttributes	10	Maximum number of Functions per operation
iterativeAlgorithmThreshold	10	Threshold for the iterative algorithm
poolInputOutputAttributes	12	Number of potential values for an input or output attribute
poolCategoryAttributes	12	Number of potential values for the Category attribute
poolFunctionAttributes	12	Number of potential values for the Function attribute
nbrQoWS	5	Number of QoWS parameters
nbrNegativeQoWS	2	Number of negative QoWS parameters
nbrPositiveQoWS	3	Number of positive QoWS parameters

Figure 5.7 presents the experimental results obtained for the *bi-selection algorithm*. As we see from the chart, the behavior of the algorithm is similar to the one obtained in the analytical study.

Figure 5.8 presents the experimental results obtained for the *iterative-selection algorithm* in its first form. As we see from the chart, the behavior of the algorithm is similar to the one obtained in the analytical study.

Figure 5.9 presents the experimental results obtained for the *simulate annealing algorithm*. As we see from the chart, the behavior of the algorithm is similar to the one obtained in the analytical study.

In the following experiment (Figure 5.10), we compare the processing time for the three algorithms: *bi-selection*, *iterative* (first form), and *simulated annealing*. The *bi-selection* and *iterative* algorithms have comparable processing times, while the *simulated annealing* spends a much greater time to find a solution. This is predictable as the annealing tries to attain an equilibrium state through several loops.

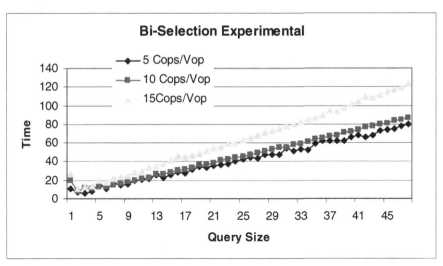

Fig. 5.7 Bi-Selection Algorithm

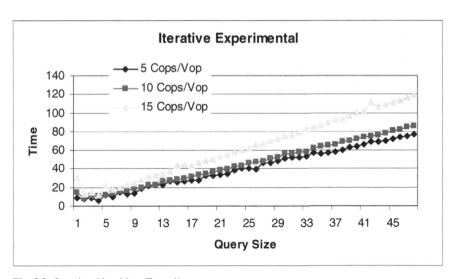

Fig. 5.8 Iterative Algorithm (Form 1)

In the last experiments (Figure 5.11), we compare the value of the aggregated cost (objective function) of the three algorithms: *bi-selection*, *iterative* (first form), and *simulated annealing*. The *bi-selection* and *iterative* algorithms achieve similar results. Surprisingly, the *simulated annealing algorithm* achieves poor results. This

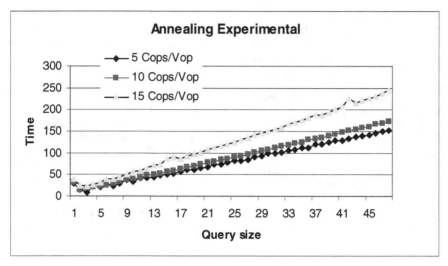

Fig. 5.9 Simulated Annealing Algorithm

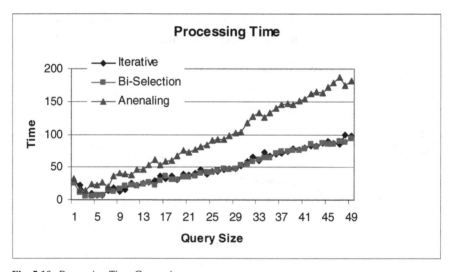

Fig. 5.10 Processing Time Comparison

may be due to the perturbation procedure that is causing the current solution to
diverge from an optimal solution.

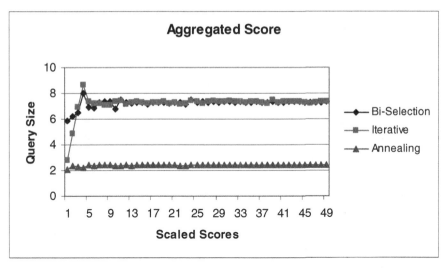

Fig. 5.11 Aggregated Costs Comparison

Chapter 6
Current Advances in Semantic Web Services and Web Databases

Abstract The work we presented in this book relates to several research areas including Web databases integration and efficient querying, as well as Web service querying, composition, and optimization. A review of these different areas as they relate to this book are discussed in this chapter.

In this chapter, we survey query processing and optimization in *Web database integration systems* [75] and Web services. A major difficulty in optimizing queries on the Web is that once a query is submitted to a specific information source, control over its execution is no longer possible. Further compounding this problem, these information sources may exhibit a different behavior from what has been initially assumed, thus impairing predictions. As a result, traditional optimization techniques that rely heavily on statistical information may be hardly applicable. Query optimization on the Web may also span a larger spectrum of criteria than those in the classical cost model. Such an example is the *information quality* criterion that codifies reliability and availability of sources, fees, etc. Furthermore, the Web's volatility and highly dynamic nature are a challenge when the expectation is that queries always return results. Further, not all information sources are expected to provide the same *query capabilities*. The query processor needs to make sure that the generated query execution plan is *feasible* with respect to these limitations.

We also present a classification of the different presented techniques and a comprehensive framework to evaluate them [75]. Most of the described systems adopt the mediator approach [95] for data integration. Those are systems that match information requests from consumers, individual users or applications, to information providers. This chapter classifies the different systems according to the focus of their query optimization approaches. We overview cost-based optimization techniques, adaptive query optimization, quality-based optimization, and query optimization in presence of sources with limited capabilities. In general, cost-based optimization techniques extend the classical cost model through various means such as estimation, caching, etc. Adaptive schemes addresses efficiency in presence of unpredictable events. Quality-based optimization takes a different direction regarding what matters more in terms of optimization on the Web. Finally, the last group of techniques focuses on optimizing queries while making sure that their execution is possible.

As it will be highlighted in this chapter, providing efficient access to interconnected databases and other information sources received a sustained interest. Several approaches and techniques have been proposed to deal with the various issues. These issues are particularly challenging due the characteristics of the Web, including amounts of Web data, large heterogeneity spectrum, strict autonomy, and volatility. In this section, we shed the light on the major paradigm shift that is taking place on the Web through the two concepts of *Semantic Web* and *Web services*. We believe that this paradigm shift would have an important impact on the issue of data integration and subsequently on query processing and optimization over the Web. While classical data integration is still relevant in some specific domains, providing query facilities over Web services covers a broader scope.

The Web is geared towards an important paradigm shift through the concept of *Semantic Web* [19]. This basically means a transition from documents for human consumption to documents with machine-processable semantics. Allowing machine-processable content would be mainly based via another new paradigm shift, namely *Web services* [18]. A Web Service is a piece of software that can be defined, described and discovered by XML artifacts (http://www.w3c.org/2002/ws). Enabling efficient access over this plethora of services is an emerging research challenge for tomorrow's *Semantic Web*. Interacting with Web resources (e.g., databases, XML data stores, etc.) is taking a new direction with the emergence of *Web services*. Web services are gaining momentum and starting to be widely used for diverse activities on the Web. The use of Web services offer new perspectives in addressing issues related to querying the Web. It opens the door for a broader view of information integration on the Web.

An important future direction is to build a *query infrastructure* where Web services would be treated as *first class objects*. Users and applications would submit queries that are resolved by combining invocations to several Web service operations. The surge of research in Web services is due to several reasons that make them an attractive alternative to data-centric approaches. First, the ongoing standardization efforts to describe, publish, search, and invoke Web services have been instrumental in their emergence. Second, Web Services are becoming ubiquitous; access to Web resources, including Web databases, is mainly achieved through Web services. This makes Web services an ideal candidate for enabling querying on the Web. Hence, the Web is evolving from a passive medium for publishing data into a more active platform for conducting business. As a result, there is a need to build an infrastructure to organize and efficiently query Web services where they would be treated as *first-class* objects [74].

The remainder of this chapter is organized as follows. Section 2 summarizes early work on query optimization in the pre-Web era. It also briefly outlines some basic query optimization principles. Section 3 introduces data integration on the Web and a thorough presentation of research issues for query optimization in this context. Section 4 describes different systems and techniques for query optimization on Web data integration systems. These are covered in four parts according to their focus. Section 5 provides a summary and discussion of the different data-centric approaches. We then move in Section 6 to discuss recent research on Web services that has some overlapping with our proposed query infrastructure.

6.1 Web Databases Integration and Efficient Querying

The advent of the Web has brought to the fore the seamless interconnection of diverse and large numbers of information sources. Allowing *uniform* querying of those sources has been a major goal of several research efforts. Most proposed systems and techniques focused on making such uniform querying feasible despite all types of hurdles (e.g., heterogeneity, autonomy, and unpredictability of the Web.) However, achieving the full potential of uniformly querying disparate Web information sources is fundamentally dependent on devising adequate query optimization techniques.

Different approaches have been used for Web-based data integration. The most widely used approach is based on the concept of *mediator* initially introduced [95]. Most of the systems and techniques in this chapter fall into that category. There are also other approaches based on the use of agents [70], ontology [6, 72, 63], and information retrieval techniques [56, 64, 9]. This section starts by an historical note about pre-Web data integration efforts. It then gives some details about the mediator approach. Finally, it highlights major research issues related to query optimization for data integration on the Web.

6.1.1 Pre-Web Data Integration

We briefly outline, in this section, major work conducted in database integration and query optimization in the pre-Web era. We first summarize some basic concepts on query optimization. We then overview the main data integration approaches and how query optimization is addressed.

Given a declarative query, e.g., in SQL, there are several execution plans that can be used to produce its results. These different plans answer the same query and are equivalent in terms of their final output. However, they may differ according to different performance parameters like response time and resource use. Researchers have recognized the importance of designing a module that would select the "best" query execution plan. Optimization has received a particular attention in the database arena and several techniques have been proposed.

The role of the optimizer is to determine a *query execution plan* that minimizes an *objective cost function*. The optimization problem can be described abstractly as follows [38]: Given a query Q, an execution space E that computes Q, and a cost function c defined over E, find an execution e in E_Q (the subset of E that computes Q) of minimum cost: $[min_{e \in E_Q} c(e)]$. An optimizer can be characterized by three dimensions [78]: (i) *Execution space* that captures the underlying execution model and defines the alternative executions. (ii) *Cost model* to predict the cost of an execution, and (iii) *Search strategy* that enumerates the execution plans and select the best one. Traditional query optimization strategies have been classified in three main categories [78]:

- *Heuristic-based* – Heuristic rules are used to *re-arrange* the different operations in a query execution plan. For example, to minimize the size of intermediate results.
- *Cost-based* – The cost of different strategies are estimated and the best one is selected in order to minimize the objective cost function. For example, the number of I/Os.
- *Hybrid* – Heuristic rules and cost estimates are combined together.

In most cases, the focus is on the *join* operation which is the most costly operation.

Data Integration Approaches

Information systems that provide interoperation and varying degrees of integration among multiple databases have been termed multidatabase systems [53], federated databases [50], and more generally *heterogeneous distributed database systems* (HDDBS). *Data integration* generally implies *uniform* and *transparent* access to data managed by multiple databases. A mechanism to achieve that goal is through an integrated schema that involves all or parts of the component schemas. The taxonomy presented by [86] classifies the existing solutions in three categories: *global schema integration*, *federated databases*, and *multidatabase language approach*. These categories are presented according to how tightly integrated component systems are.

Global schema integration was one of the first attempts at data sharing across HDDBS. It is based on the complete integration of multiple databases to provide a single view (global schema) [87]. In [13], an exhaustive survey on schema integration is provided along with a comparison of several methodologies. In federated databases [50], a certain amount of autonomy for individual database systems is maintained. Information sharing occurs through *import* and *export* schemas. A particular database exports part of or the whole schema depending on which database it is exporting to. The importing database has to perform any needed integration locally. All databases are registered in a federal dictionary.

The *multidatabase language* approach is intended for users who do not use a predefined global or partial schema. Preexisting heterogeneous local databases are usually integrated without modifications. Information stored in different databases may be redundant, heterogeneous, and inconsistent. The aim of a multidatabase language is to provide constructs that perform queries involving several databases at the same time. One major criticism of this approach is the lack of distribution and location transparency, as users have to *a priori* find the right information in a potentially large network of databases. Users are responsible for understanding schemas, and detecting and resolving semantic conflicts. In this approach, users are faced with the issues that consist of *finding* the relevant information in multiple databases, *understanding* each individual database schema, *detecting* and *resolving* semantic conflicts, and *performing* view integration.

Query Optimization

Query optimization has received a particular attention in heterogeneous distributed databases systems. It was noted early on that the lack of statistical information from participating databases prevented a direct application of techniques developed for homogeneous systems. Different techniques have been proposed to overcome the lack of statistical information. For example, Pegasus [85] uses a cost model based on logical parameters that include database cardinality and selectivity. These parameters are obtained using calibrating queries. If they cannot be calculated, a number of heuristics are used to optimize queries. In CORDS [100], sampling and probing are applied to local databases to estimate costs by gathering statistical information. Some special queries are executed on top of the participating databases and their behavior and results are recorded. This process is repeated as frequently as needed. Query processing at the global level is then conducted using the gathered information along with a classical cost-based model. Another example is MIND [77]. It uses a dynamic optimization strategy. A statistical scheme is used at runtime to determine and select the less costly and more selective inter-site operation between currently available partial results. Each inter-site operation is assigned with a weight that includes its cost, selectivity, and transfer cost. Operations are scheduled if their weights do not exceed a threshold value computed each time a partial result is available.

6.1.2 Mediator-based Approaches

Mediators provide an *integrated view* or *mediated schema* over multiple heterogeneous and autonomous information sources. This schema represents generally a *synthesized view* over a specific application domain. Users access the integrated view through a uniform interface that offers *location*, *model*, and *interface transparency*. In general, each source is connected to a *wrapper* that enables its participation in the system. It translates between the source's local language, model, and concepts and those at the mediator level.

To resolve a query, a mediator typically performs three main tasks [48]:

- *Database selection* – Locate and select the databases that are relevant to the query.

- *Query translation* – Decompose the query into sub-queries with respect to the previously selected databases. Each sub-query is transformed into a form that is executable by the corresponding database. The sub-query is then sent to the database (through a wrapper) and results are retrieved.
- *Result merging* – Combine the different results into a global answer to the user.

An important characterization of mediator systems relates to the nature of the relationship between the *mediated schema* and the schemas of participating databases. Two main approaches have been adopted [39]: In the *source-centric* (a.k.a. *local-as-view*) approach, relations stored by the information sources are described in terms of the global schema. In the *query-centric* (a.k.a. *global-as-view*) approach, the global schema is defined in terms of the relations stored by the local information sources. The source-centric approach scales better than the query-centric since modifications at the information sources do not affect the rest of the system. On the other hand, translating global queries into local ones is easier in the query-centric approach.

6.1.3 Research Issues

Query optimization has received a particular attention in different types of database systems (e.g., central, distributed, and multidatabase). Indeed, the ultimate goal of any database system is to allow efficient querying. Unsurprisingly, data integration systems over the Web does not escape to that objective. Query optimization is also central to the deployment of data integration systems overs the Web. It has been deemed as more challenging due to the very nature of the Web (large heterogeneity spectrum, strict autonomy, large user base, dynamic behavior, etc.) Queries over Web information sources may be answered in various ways. Each alternative outputs usually the same results. However, alternatives may differ widely in terms of efficiency. This may relate to response time, network resources, number of information sources involved, quality of the information being accessed, quality of returned results, users' satisfaction, and so on. Consequently, query optimization techniques for the Web need to be carefully crafted. Devising the right techniques would necessitate to address a large spectrum of issues. In the following, we outline issues that are directly related to query optimization over data integration systems on the Web.

Optimization paradigm

Optimizing queries amounts usually to minimizing the response time. This is the objective function driving most optimizers. Although, this is still desirable on the Web, some applications may require the use of different parameters in the objective function. These include fees to access informations sources, quality of the data (e.g., freshness), number of sources to access, etc. Devising an optimizer requires to first set up an adequate objective function that is relevant to Web applications.

Optimizing over a large number of heterogeneous and autonomous information sources

Data integration faces a far more incongruent environment than in the pre-Web era. Heterogeneity can happen at different levels of the data integration system. The time and resources required to bridge that heterogeneity may have an important impact on the optimization process. Autonomy, has a more serious impact since several optimization techniques require specific information from information sources. This information is not always easily available. Furthermore, once a (sub-)query is submitted to a specific information source, the optimizer of the data integration system does not have any control over it. Finally, the Web is witnessing an exponential growth in terms of information sources and potential users. Query optimization should take into account scalability issues to avoid performance degradation. This degradation could lead to very inefficient query execution plans.

Evolving in a dynamic environment

A major characteristic of the Web lies in its high dynamism and volatility. Information sources availability and behavior can change without warning. In addition, unpredictable events could happen anytime during query processing and execution. The query optimizer would need adaptive mechanisms to avoid missing optimal query execution in the occurrence of any event. Adaptive techniques could be also used to gather optimization information *on the fly* and use them to modify the execution plan.

Dealing with limited query capabilities

Web information sources do not generally exhibit the same capabilities in terms of the queries that they can handle. These limitations are due to several reasons including performance and security. They may range from fully featured database systems allowing full access to their content to information sources with restricted access forms. The query optimizer must generate efficient query execution plans that are effectively executable with respect to any constraint imposed by the accessed sources. This may especially mean that some optimal plans are skipped since they are not feasible.

Locating sources of interest

Queries do not generally specify the specific information sources that need to be accessed. In some cases, finding those sources is a straightforward process, e.g., *query unfolding* in global-as-view based mediators. While in others it is more challenging. More precisely, the query optimizer should be able to limit access to only: (1) relevant sources to avoid wasting resources, and (2) sources with superior qualities if alternative sources compete in offering the same information. Addressing this issue is dependent on how much meta-information is available about information sources. This relates to the issue of source description and advertisement.

6.1.4 Dimensions for Query Optimization on the Web

In surveying research conducted on query optimization in Web data integration systems, we noticed that there is a lack of a comparison of the different approaches. That situation is due to the lack of an analytical model to compare those techniques. In classical systems, well established models and benchmark tools have been developed for such purpose. In the following, we propose dimensions along which query optimization for Web-based data integration systems are compared. Some of these dimensions are subjective and may not be precisely quantified.

- *Scalability* – This dimension measures the *degradation*, if any, of the query optimization technique, when the number of information sources grows. Growth could be in terms of information sources and users. This dimension may be difficult to measure in a real setting. Fine tuning may be necessary.
- *Autonomy preservation* – This relates to how much information is required from the information source for deploying the optimization technique.
- *Optimization performance* – This dimension should provide performance evaluation of the objective function under different scenarios. Scenarios may be varied based on the types of queries being submitted, the number and types of sources being accessed, and other parameters. Both analytical and experimental studies need to be conducted. Note that only very few approaches have done such studies.
- *Adaptiveness* – This reflects the ability of the optimization technique to take into account unexpected changes.
- *Capabilities* – This dimension is for checking whether the optimization technique takes into account sources with different and limited query capabilities. There is a need also to check that the technique does not miss optimal plans.

6.1.5 Cost-based Optimization

Several Web-based data integration systems have based query optimization on extending the classical cost model. A major challenge for such approach relates to optimization information from autonomous information sources. All approaches assume either such statistics are available, can be estimated, or provided by wrappers.

Disco

Disco [90] is a mediator system based on the global-as-view approach. The mediator generates multiple access plans involving local operations at the information sources and global operations at the mediator level. The data model is based on the ODMG standard. The object definition language is extended to allow multiple *extents* to be associated with an interface type of the mediator. It also provides type mapping information between a mediator and a data source.

Disco uses a cost based optimization approach [67]. It combines a *generic cost model* with specific cost information exported by wrappers. The generic cost model uses *cost formulas* established by the *calibrating approach* developed in the IRO-DB federated system [46]. The data source interface is specified using a subset of CORBA IDL extended with a *cardinality section* for data source statistics and a *cost formula section* for specific formulas. The wrapper writer exports statistics (e.g., cardinality of a collection), size rules (reflect the change in result sizes due to an operation), and cost computation rules (compute cost estimates). A query is optimized by estimating the cost of single operations and entire plans. The mediator selects the most specific information available from wrappers and the generic cost model. The cost of the execution of a query plan is determined in a two step bottom-up algorithm: *cost formula integration* and *cost estimation*. In the first step, wrapper rules are integrated into the mediator cost model. In the second step, cost estimates for a plan are generated. The plan is represented as a tree of operator nodes. It is traversed from the root to the leaves and then from the leaves to the root. In the first traversal, cost formulas are associated with nodes. In the second traversal, the cost of each operator is computed.

Garlic

Garlic [82, 49] provides an integrated view over heterogeneous information sources using the global-as-view approach. Query processing is based on dynamically determining the middleware and wrapper roles in answering a query. A wrapper provides several tasks including: (1) modeling information sources as Garlic objects, (2) allowing Garlic to retrieve references to these object, (3) allowing Garlic to invoke methods on objects and retrieve attributes, (4) participating in query processing and execution. Garlic objects have an interface that abstractly describes the object's behavior and a corresponding implementation that provides a concrete realization. A query is translated into a tree of operators or POPs (Plan OPerators). Each operator corresponds to a runtime operator, e.g., join, sort, fetch, and scan. Garlic provides also a generic POP, called PushDown POP, which encapsulates work to be conducted at a information source. Each plan is characterized by properties such as tables used in the plan, output columns, and estimated cost.

Garlic extends the traditional cost-based optimization approach by involving wrappers as important components in the optimization process [81]. Wrappers cooperate in the estimation of the total cost of a given query plan. The proposed framework aims to provide the necessary means to extend the traditional cost-based optimization to a heterogeneous environment. The framework includes a *cost model*, *cost formulas*, and *statistics*. Wrappers may use a default cost model or a more specific one to model their execution strategies. The default cost model considers the total cost of a POP operator as a combination of the cost of two basic tasks: *reset* for initializing the operator and *advance* for retrieving the next result. Default cost formulas are used to compute these two costs based on statistics. Based on the cost of the *reset* and *advance* tasks, the wrapper should be able to provide cost estimates for its own plans that are included in the global query plan. The *total cost, re-execution cost*, and *result cardinality* are considered in the cost of a PushDown POP. They are required to estimate the cost of the global query plan. Once the optimizer selects a winning plan, that plan is translated into an executable form. Garlic POPs are translated into operators that can be directly executed by the Garlic execution engine.

Ariadne

Ariadne [7] is an integration system that uses the local-as-view mediation approach. The *LOOM* knowledge representation system [58] is used to construct the domain model that represents an integrated view of the sources. User queries are formulated against that model. Query processing has two phases: a *preprocessing phase* and a *query planning phase*. A *source selection* algorithm pre-processes the domain model allowing the selection of sources based on classes and attributes. Query planning is a combination of source selection strategy and traditional distributed query optimization. It first generates an initial plan (eventually suboptimal) and then applies *rewriting rules* in order to improve the quality of the plan. These rewriting rules are iteratively applied until either an acceptable solution is found or a resource limit is reached. The quality of a query plan is based on a classical cost model depending on the size of intermediate results, cost of relational operations, and communication costs. The authors assume the availability of some statistics from the underlying sources to compute these costs. Three classes of rewriting rules are then considered. The first class of rules is derived from the properties of the distributed environment and contains four rules. One rule is based on the use of alternative information sources that can answer the same query but with different costs. The three other rules allow the execution of a group of operations in remote sources instead of transferring the data and executing the operations at a local source. The second class of rules is derived from some properties of the relational algebra (e.g., commutativity, associativity, etc.) The last class of rewriting rules relates to the heterogeneity of the environment. They are needed to reconcile the semantic differences between sources. The idea is to use axioms that describe how attributes and classes can be obtained by combining information from a set of sources.

Hermes

Hermes [4] considers the construction of mediators based on two major distinct tasks: *domain integration* - physical linking of the information sources, and the *semantic integration* - coherent extraction and combination of the information provided by these sources. Query optimization in Hermes is based on a cost-based model using caching [4]. Statistics of calls to the sources are locally cached in order to estimate the cost of possible execution plans. In addition, *invariants* are used to derive equivalent execution query plans. Invariants represent expressions that show possible substitutions for external domain calls. They specify which call can be substituted. First, the query processor checks the cache to see if the answer for a domain call is already stored in that cache. It then uses the invariants to substitute domain calls and check whether they are in the cache. If the invariants indicate that there is a domain call in the cache that only provides a partial list of answers, then the actual domain call may need to be performed.

Hermes optimizer has four components. The *rule rewriter* finds different possible rewritings of the original query expressed in terms of external calls. The *cache and invariant manager* maintains caches and avoids actual calls to external domain when the answer to that call is physically present in the cache. The manager uses also the invariants to find other acceptable entries in the cache. The *domain cost and statistics module* (DCSM) provides estimates of calls to external information sources. This module keeps execution time and cardinality statistics in a database and provides cost estimates to the *rule cost estimator*. Finally, the *rule cost estimator* takes the rewritten query from the rule rewriter and computes the cost of each plan by obtaining the cost estimates of individual calls to the sources from DCSM. The rule rewriter derives more than one plan for a query. Thus, the DCSM has to estimate the costs of each plan and select the best plan. Cost estimation relies on a cost vector database maintained by the DCSM. This database records cost information about domain calls as they are executed by the mediator.

6.1.6 Quality-based Optimization Techniques

Some systems have considered different parameters to be included in the cost of a query. Those parameters relate to *information quality* of sources and data. The argument is that such quality parameters are either equally or more important, in the context of the Web, than classical parameters like response time.

ObjectGlobe

ObjectGlobe's [32] data integration is centered around three types of suppliers: *data suppliers*, *function providers* for query processing operators, and *cycle providers* for operator execution. The execution of a query may involve query operators supplied by different function providers that are executed at different cycle providers and that retrieve data from different data providers. Query processing follows a multi-step strategy. First, a *lookup* service locates instances from each of the above types of suppliers that are relevant to the resolution of the query. Some cost information are also gathered during this step. In the second step, an optimal plan is built based on a cost model using the previously gathered information. In the last step, the query execution plan is distributed to relevant cycle providers and executed using an iterator model [47].

Queries for the lookup service are extracted by the parser based on *themes* and *attributes* specified in the different clauses of a query. The lookup service uses the generated queries to locate relevant resources by consulting a meta-data repository. The lookup service is also responsible to gather statistical information for the optimizer and authorization information from the different providers. Authorization information is recorded in a *compatibility matrix* that will annotate the query execution plan. The optimizer enumerates alternative query execution plans using a *System-R* [84] like dynamic algorithm. Costs of plans are estimated using information from the lookup service. If an information is missing it is set to a default value. The optimal plan is then executed by distributing it to the different cycle providers as specified in the host annotations of the plan. In addition, users can specify *quality constraints* on the execution of their query. Constraints are defined on results (e.g., size of the result), cost (i.e., how much the user is ready to pay), and time (e.g., time to first results). *QoS* management is introduced as part of the query processor. In fact, the quality constraints are treated in all the phases of querying processing. If they cannot be fulfilled, the query plan is dynamically adapted or the query is aborted. Based on that QoS concept, the optimizer's goal is to maximize the percentage of successful queries and abort any query that cannot fulfill its QoS constraints as soon as possible.

HiQIQ

HiQIQ (High Quality Information Querying) uses information quality criteria to support query optimization in mediator systems [69]. The focus is on incorporating information quality into query planning. This could be useful in environments such as biological information systems where users are more sensitive to quality criteria than the classical database criterion, i.e., response time. The approach uses a mediator based architecture where the mediator uses *query correspondence assertions* (*QCAs*) to resolve queries. *QCAs* are *set oriented equations* involving queries over mediator and wrapper schemas. This is a sort of combination of the *source-centric* and *query-centric* approaches used in mediators. The query resolution process tries to find all correct plans (combinations of *QCAs*) and then does a union over their results to obtain the complete answer.

To include *quality information* (*IQ*) in the query planning, three classes of quality criteria have been used. *Source-specific* criteria determine the overall quality of a source. They include ease of understanding, reputation, reliability, and timeliness.

QCA-specific criteria determine quality aspects of specific queries that are computable by a source. These include availability, price, response time, accuracy, relevancy and representational consistency. *Attribute-specific* criteria relate to the ability of a source to provide the attributes of a specific query. Query processing is conducted in a three phase strategy. Based on the source-specific *IQ* criteria, the first phase prunes low-quality sources. The second phase finds all plans, i.e., combinations of QCAs, that produce semantically correct answers. The query planning strategy of Information Manifold [57] (see Section 6.1.8) is used. This phase does not use any quality related information. Finally, plans obtained from the previous phase are qualitatively ranked. This phase starts by determining *IQ scores* for the different QCAs in the different plans. That score is a vector with eight dimensions; each dimension corresponding to a non-source-specific criteria (six QCA-specific and two attribute-specific). Only attribute-specific criteria are recalculated for each new query, the others are more stable. In a second step, an IQ vector is computed for each plan by merging IQ vectors in join nodes appearing in the plan. In the third and last step, IQ scores for the different plans are scaled, weighted, and compared using a simple decision making method (i.e., the simple additive weighting). This method scales the scores to make them comparable, apply the user weighting, and sum up the scores for each plan.

6.1.7 Adaptive Query Optimization

An important issue in Web-based data integration is the use of *adaptive* or *dynamic query optimization* techniques to face the high volatility of the Web. These techniques address mainly the lack of statistical information and occurrence of unpredictable events during query execution. They generally try to change the execution plan at run-time, re-optimize the query, or use specific operators that deal more flexibly with unpredictable events (e.g., data delivery rates). An interesting characterization of adaptive query processors is given in [51]. It states that a query processing is adaptive if:

- it receives information from its environment,
- it uses that information to determine its behavior, and
- this process iterates over time, generating a feedback loop between environment and behavior.

In this section, we present some major projects that use dynamic query optimization.

Telegraph

The Telegraph project [51] aims to build a query engine over Web information sources based on an adaptive *data-flow paradigm*. The objective is to adaptively route unpredictable and bursty data-flows through computing resources. The query processor continuously reorders applications of pipelined operators in a query plan at run-time on a tuple-by-tuple basis [11]. Is uses the concept of *eddy*, defined as a *n*-ary tuple router interposed between *n* data sources and a set of query processing operators.

An *eddy* encapsulates the ordering of operators by dynamically routing tuples through them. The idea is that there are times during the processing of a binary operator (e.g., join, union) where it is possible to modify the order of the inputs without modifying any state in the operator. Such times are called *moments of symmetry*. They occur at the so called *synchronization barriers*. For the case of *merge join*, this corresponds to one table-scan waiting until the other table-scan produces values larger than any one seen before. Most of the reported work for *eddies* is on the join operator due to its impact on query performance. The focus in Telegraph is on join algorithms with frequent times of symmetry, adaptive or non-existent barriers, and minimal ordering constraints. Efficiency of the system depends tightly on the routing policy used in the *eddies*. Different routing policies need to be used under different circumstances. They depends on operator selectivity, operator consumption and production rate, join implementation, and initial delays of input relations. Eddies have been implemented in the context of a shared-nothing parallel query processing framework called River [10].

Tukwila

Tukwila is another system addressing adaptiveness in data integration environment [55]. Adaptiveness is introduced at two levels: (1) between the optimizer and the execution engine, and (2) within the execution engine. In the first level, adaptiveness is deployed by annotating initial query plans by (event-condition-action) *ECA rules*. These rules check some conditions when certain events occur and subsequently trigger the execution of some actions. Examples of events include operator failure, time-out, and out of memory exceptions. Conditions include the comparison of actual cardinalities known at run-time and those estimated. Finally, actions include rescheduling of the query operator tree, re-optimization of the plan, and alteration of memory allocation. A plan is organized into a partially ordered set of fragments and a set of corresponding rules. Fragments are pipelined units of operators. When a fragment terminates, results are materialized and the rest of the plan can be re-optimized or rescheduled. In addition to data manipulation, operators perform two actions: statistics gathering for the optimizer, and event handler invocation in case a significant event occurs. The operator tree execution follows the top-down iterator model described in [47].

For the second level of adaptiveness, two operators are used: *dynamic collectors* and the *double pipelined hash join* operator. The collector operator dynamically chooses relevant sources when a union involves data from possibly overlapping or redundant sources. The optimizer specifies the order to access sources and alternative sources in case of unavailability or slow delivery. A collector will then include a set of children (wrapper calls or table-scans) and a policy for contacting them. The policy is expressed as a set of event-condition-action (ECA) rules. The double pipelined hash join is a symmetric and incremental join. It aims at producing tuples quickly and masking slow data sources transfer rates. This requires maintaining hash tables for in memory relations. The original double pipelined join has been implemented after a few adaptations. The first adaption was to retrofit the data-driven bottom-up execution model of that operator with the Tukwila's query processing top-down iterator-based scheme. The second relates to the problem of memory overflow. Two strategies based on swapping are used.

Interleaving Scheduling and Optimization

Another dynamic scheduling strategy that deals also with memory limitation has been proposed in [21]. It is based on monitoring arrival rates at the information sources and memory availability. In the case of significant changes, the execution plan is revised. This means that planning and execution phases are interleaved. The query execution plan is represented by an operator tree with two particular edges: *blocking* and *pipelinable*. In a *blocking edge*, the consumption of data cannot start before it is entirely produced. In a *pipelinable edge*, data can be consumed one tuple at a time meaning that consumption can start as soon as one tuple is available. It is then possible to characterize the query execution plan by pipelinable chains which represent the maximal set of physical operators linked by pipelinable edges. The query engine will have to concurrently select, schedule, and execute several query fragments (pipelinable chains and partial materializations) while minimizing the response time.

The query engine's main components are the *dynamic query optimizer*, *dynamic query scheduler*, *dynamic query processor*, and *communication manager*. The dynamic query optimizer uses dynamic re-optimization techniques to generate an annotated query execution plan. Those annotations relate to blocking and pipelinable edges, memory requirements, and estimates of results' sizes. The dynamic query scheduler builds a scheduling plan at each scheduling phase triggered by events from the query processor. Scheduling is based on some heuristics, the current execution status, and information about the benefits of materialization of pipelinable chains. The dynamic query processor concurrently processes query fragments while maximizing the processor use based on priorities defined in the scheduled plan. The execution may be interrupted in case there is no data arriving from sources, a query fragment has ended, or delivery rates have significantly changed. This is reported to the query scheduler and eventually to the query optimizer for scheduling or optimization changes. The communication manager receives data from the different wrappers for the rest of the system. It also estimates delivery rates at the sources and reports significant changes to the query processor.

Query Scrambling

A *query scrambling* approach is proposed in [8]. The goal is to react to delays by modifying the query execution plan *on-the-fly*. Unexpected delays are "hidden" by performing other useful works. Scrambling has a two-pronged action: *rescheduling* (scheduling other operators for execution) and *operator synthesis* (new operators are created when there is no other operator to execute). These two techniques are repeated as necessary to modify the query execution plan. Scrambling policies differ by the degree of parallelism they introduce or the aggressiveness with which scrambling changes the existing query plan. Three important trade-offs must be considered in *rescheduling*: First, the number of operators to reschedule concurrently. This concerns the benefits of overlapping multiple delays and the cost of materializations used to achieve this overlapping. Second, rescheduling individual operators or entire subtrees. Finally, choice of specific operator(s) to reschedule. For *operator synthesis*, a significant amount of additional work may be added since the operations were not originally chosen by the optimizer. To avoid this problem a simple heuristic of avoiding Cartesian products to prevent the creation of overly expensive joins is used. However, the performance of this heuristic is highly sensitive to the cardinality of the new operators created.

6.1.8 Optimizing Queries over Sources with Limited Capabilities

Building mediators involves dealing with sources presenting different capabilities in terms of the queries they can handle. This scenario is likely to occur on the Web, where sources adhering to specific requirements and constraints limit access through some patterns. For example, users of an online bookstore get information on books via forms. These forms allow several types of keyword based queries including search by title, subject, author, keyword, ISBN, etc. However, a user cannot submit database-like queries using complex conditions on prices or requesting all available books. There are several reasons for limiting the query capabilities of an information source. These include:

- *Performance* – Only some types of queries are allowed to maintain the performance of the system. For example, allowing conditions on only attributes that have indexes.
- *Security* – Supported queries cannot access privileged information.
- *Legacy* – The underlying data may actually be stored in systems with limited query capabilities.
- *Business* – Queries that can retrieve useful business information, e.g., using aggregate queries, are not allowed.

In this section, we present some techniques that have been developed to deal with this problem, i.e., how to efficiently answer queries over sources with limited capabilities.

Tsimmis

Tsimmis prototype [45] integrates heterogeneous information sources using the global-as-view approach for mediation. The proposed mediation is supported through a number of concepts. An object model called *OEM* (*Object–Exchange Model*) is used to exchange information between components of the system. A *Mediator Specification Language* (*MSL*) based on OEM serves as the query language, the specification language for mediators, and the query language for wrappers. Capabilities of sources are described using *templates*. OEM is a self-describing object data model, i.e., data can be parsed without reference to an external schema. Templates represent the set of queries that are *answerable* by each source. Generally speaking, a query is *answerable* if it provides all inputs required by the source. The capability descriptions of sources are used to decide on the feasibility of physical query plans.

Query resolution in Tsimmis focuses mainly on finding *feasible query plans* that respect the limited capabilities of available sources. A user query is initially expressed against an integrated view. The *view expander* module (in the mediator) translates the query into a *logical plan* using the *view definitions*. Such logical plan does not specify the order in which source queries are processed. Processing order is specified in the *physical plan* which may in turn may have several alternatives. The plan generator processes the logical plan and generates an optimized feasible physical plan in a three step process. First, the *matcher* finds all source queries that can process parts of the logical plan based on the source descriptions. Second, the *sequencer* pieces together the source queries for processing the conditions of the logical plan to build feasible plans. It has to find a feasible sequence of source queries. For example, a query in a feasible sequence has the property that its binding requirements are exported by the source queries that appear earlier in the sequence. Finally, the *optimizer* chooses the most efficient feasible plan using a cost based optimization algorithm.

Information Manifold

Information Manifold [57] provides a uniform interface to structured information sources. It proposes a mechanism to describe *declaratively* the content and query capabilities of information sources. The system uses the source descriptions to prune sources for a given query and generate executable query plans. Sources' content is described by queries over a set of relations and classes. Users express their queries against a mediated view consisting of a collection of *virtual relations* and *classes*. Relations are described in the sources as *queries* over the *world view relations*. Thus, Information Manifold follows a *local-as-view* approach for mediation.

The execution plan for a query Q is generated using a two-phase algorithm. In the *first phase*, a *semantically correct plan* is generated. It is a *conjunctive* query Q' that uses only source relations and is contained in the user query Q. First, for each *subgoal* in the query, the algorithm computes a *bucket* containing the information sources from which tuples of that subgoal can be obtained. After that, all possible combinations of information sources, one from each *bucket*, are considered. The obtained plan is checked for semantic correctness. For each subgoal in the query, relevant information sources are computed separately. Conjunctive plans are then built by selecting one relevant source for every subgoal in the query. Each plan is checked for *relevance* and *soundness*. A conjunctive plan is *sound* if all the answers it produces are guaranteed to be answers to the query. A conjunctive plan is *relevant* if it can produce answers to the query according to the descriptions of the sources and the constraints in the query. In the last step of the first phase, each plan is checked for *minimality*. This ensures that if a subgoal is removed from the plan then the plan is not sound anymore. The *second phase* orders subgoals such that the plan is executable with respect to the capabilities of sources. The algorithm generates the ordering based on possible *bindings*. It maintains a list of available parameters initialized by the set of bound variables in the query. A subgoal is added to the ordering if its input requirements are satisfied with respect to the list of available parameters and source requirements, and it was not already considered.

Infomaster

Infomaster [40] provides integrated access to distributed heterogeneous information sources, including databases and semistructured data. Infomaster uses the knowledge interchange format (KIF) as an internal content language. KIF is used to represent first order logic expressions. The Infomaster system follows the *source–centric* approach for mediation. Infomaster considers three types of relations. First, *interface relations* are used by users to formulate queries. Second, the *source relations* describe the data stored in the information sources. Both relations are described using a third type, *world relations*, that represents a reference schema for the system.

Query optimization is based on the notion of *local completeness* that limits the number of sources to be queried. Infomaster uses a weak form of completeness that assumes that some subset of the data stored by an information source is complete. This is assumed even if the entire data stored by this information source might not be complete. The claim is that such assumption is reasonable within a specific application domain. In this approach, any source relation is represented by two views over the global relations. The *liberal view* and *conservative view*. These two views have the same schema as the corresponding source relation. The conservative view is a *lower bound* of the source relation and describes the subset of the data that is known to be complete. The liberal view is an *upper bound* of the source relation. Based on conservative and liberal views of the different information sources, the query processor generates a query plan that is: (1) *retrievable*, (2) *semantically correct*, (3) *source complete*, and (4) *view minimal*. The query processor generates such plans in a five step algorithm. (1) *Reduction*: The query is transformed in terms of base relations by rewriting each atom using definition of the associated predicates. (2) *Abduction*: Given the expression Q_b in terms of base relations and a set of definitions, the set of all consistent and minimal conjunctions and retrievable atoms is produced. This set is contained in Q_b with respect to the given definition. (3) *Conjunctive minimization*: Any redundant conjunct is eliminated. (4) Disjunctive minimization: Any disjunct that can be shown to be contained in the union of the remaining disjuncts is discarded. (5) *Grouping*: The conjuncts within each conjunction are grouped so that the atoms in each group share a common provider.

Annotated Query Plans

The approach proposed in [43] extends the *System-R* optimizer to deal with sources having limited query capabilities. It uses *annotated query plans* in the search space. Annotations describe the *input* that *must* be given to each sub-plan in the query plan to be *answerable*. The proposed algorithm aims to prune invalid and non-viable plans as early as possible and uses a best-first search strategy to produce a complete plan early in the search. Limitations of sources are modeled through binding patterns. A binding pattern specifies which attributes must be *bound*, i.e., have an input value, in order to retrieve tuples from a relation. Each binding pattern is also labeled with the cost of accessing it once and cardinality of the expected output per given input. The cost of a sub-plan is computed based on these costs and the cost of the associated operator. The approach assumes *select-project-join* queries or *conjunctive* queries. The goal is then to find the cheapest complete query execution plan for a conjunctive query q given a set of binding patterns. A *complete* query execution plan is a plan that covers all the conjuncts in the query and whose *adornment* maps precisely the bound variables in the query to *bound*. Atomic plan costs are deduced from the data access descriptions. Non-atomic plan costs are estimated based on the costs of the operators and the costs of the sub-plans.

The query optimization algorithm starts by an initial set S of plans containing only atomic plans, i.e., single relations. S is then iteratively updated by adding new plans obtained by combining plans from S using selection and join operations. The choice of the partial plans to be combined is based on a *utility* measure. The *utility* measure is based on the number of conjuncts covered by a plan, cost of the plans, number of free variables, or a combination thereof. During the combination of partial plans, pruning occurs by comparing the costs of equivalent plans and the costs of *covering plans*. A plan p_1 covers another plan p_2 if they are labeled with the same set of conjuncts from the query and p_1 may need less variables to be bound than p_2 (p_2 is equivalent to a *selection* applied to p_1.) At the end of the iteration, two cases can occur. In the first case, S contains the *equivalence class* of the query and thus the optimal plan. In the second case, further processing is needed to get the optimal plan. The algorithm applies an exhaustive enumeration of all possible placements of selections in the obtained plans. This process leads to the optimal plan.

Source Sequencing Algorithms

In [96], a simple *greedy strategy* and a *partitioning scheme* are proposed to deal with limited capabilities of sources. Both algorithms use a cost model based on the number of source queries in the execution plan. Users submit conjunctive queries over integrated views provided by a mediator. Each integrated view is defined as a set of conjunctive queries over the source relations. Each source relation defines a set of access templates that specify the binding requirements.

The first algorithm starts by finding all answerable subgoals using the initial bindings in the logical plan, and picks the one with the least cost. The selected subgoal will then provide additional bound variables. Thus, the process is repeated by selecting the *cheapest* subgoals and updating the set of bound variables. The process stops when there is no more subgoals or none of the left subgoals is answerable. It is clear that such greedy approach may miss the optimal plan.

The second algorithm generates optimal plans more frequently than the first but has a worse running time. It has two phases: In the first phase, subgoals are organized into a list of clusters based on source capabilities. All the subgoals in the first cluster are answerable by block queries (i.e., queries that use only initially bound variables) and all other are answerable by parameterized queries (i.e., queries that use variable bindings from the subgoals of earlier clusters). In the second phase, the algorithm finds the best sub-plans for each cluster and then combines them to obtain the best feasible plan for the query.

Capability Sensitive Plans for Selection Queries

In [44], two algorithms for generating plans for *selection queries* over Web data sources are presented. Sources exhibit restrictions on the size and structure of condition expressions along with limitations on the set of returned attributes. Sources are described using a context free language. Queries are of the form $\pi_A(\sigma_C(R))$ and are noted by *SP(C, A, R)*. The selection condition C is represented by a condition tree. *Leaf nodes* represent atomic conditions without any disjunctive or conjunctive conditions. *Non-leaf nodes* represent Boolean connectors $\wedge$ and $\vee$. Mediator query plans are represented by query trees. Leaf nodes represent *SP* source queries and non leaf nodes represent selection, projection, union, and intersection operations. These operations are performed at the mediator level to combine results from source queries.

The first algorithm is a simple exhaustive modular scheme that has four modules: *rewrite, mark, generate*, and *cost*. The *rewrite* module produces a set of equivalent rewritings for the target query condition. It employs a number of rules including *commutative, associative*, and *distributive* transformations of condition expressions. The *rewrite* module outputs a set of *condition trees* (CTs) that represent the condition expressions of the query. For each condition tree produced by the *rewrite* module, the *mark* module determines the parts that can be evaluated at the source. If the condition is not supported by the source, the *generate* module produces a set of *feasible* plans by repeatedly invoking the *Exhaustive Plan Generator* (EPG) algorithm on each of the *CTs* passed on by the *mark* module. *EPG* is a recursive algorithm that generates a feasible plan for a query *SP(n,A,R)*. If *EPG* finds feasible plans, it represents them using a special operator to indicate alternative query plans for *SP(n,A,R)*. Finally, the *cost* module selects the best plan using a cost model.

The second scheme improves the first one by reducing the number of *CTs* that need to be processed and the search space using some knowledge about the cost model. As a result, the *Rewrite* module triggers a fewer number of rules. The commutativity rule is included in the source description itself and is not triggered. This requires rewriting the source descriptions and parsing a larger set of rules. This overhead occurs only once and should not have much impact on performance. The cost of querying a source consists of: (1) the overhead of sending messages and starting a query, (2) the cost of computing the answer at the source, and (3) the cost of transferring results over the network. Based on this cost model, three pruning rules are used to reduce the search space: (1) prune *impure* plans when *pure* plan exist, a *pure* plan process the entire query at the source, (2) prune locally sub-optimal plans, when decomposing an *impure* plan into sub-queries and choose only sub-queries with the least cost, and (3) prune *dominated* plans, i.e., plans with a more expensive cost than other plans on the same relation and attributes, and whose condition includes the condition of the expensive plan (this can only be applied for conjunctive conditions).

6.1.9 Discussions

Enabling data integration on the Web and the subsequent need for efficient querying have been targeted by a large research effort. In this chapter, we presented a representative segment of that research. The following discussion outlines how the various query optimization issues have been addressed. Figure 6.1 depicts a classification of different approaches for optimizing queries over Web data integration systems. The figure highlights four categories of query optimization techniques in the context of Web-based data integration. These are cost-based, quality-based, capability-based, and adaptive. For each category, the figure lists the main features of different techniques used to implement query optimizers in that category.

Some of the proposed approaches extend the classical cost model. A major difficulty relates to gathering optimization information (e.g., cardinality, selectivity) from autonomous information sources. Some approaches (e.g., Disco) simply make the assumption that such information is (easily) available from the sources or exported by the wrappers. Others (e.g., Garlic) provide wrapper builders with tools to gather such information (e.g., query sampling) without requiring the involvement of the database. For the two above approaches, if the cost information cannot be obtained, a generic model is generally used. Using a generic model may not be always applicable in the Web context with a large spectrum of autonomous and heterogeneous information sources. In addition, making the assumption that statistics are

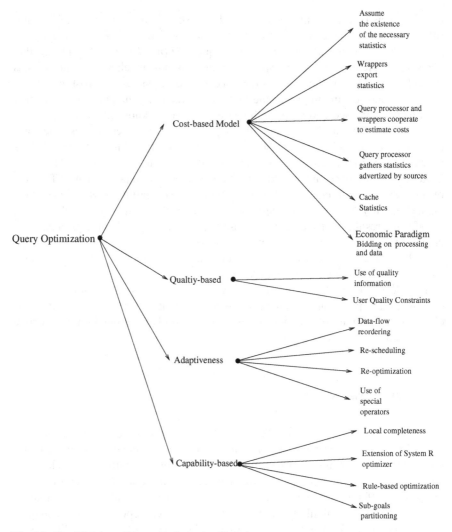

Fig. 6.1 Classification of Query Optimization Techniques

available or can be easily obtained may not be always reasonable. This suggests that most of the techniques may be more appropriate for intranet-like applications.

For some systems, the main objective in terms of optimization is to reduce the number of sources to be accessed. Sources reduction occurs at query planning time (e.g., Infomaster) based on available source descriptions and the user query, and at run time using some special types of queries (e.g., Ariadne). Reducing the number of sources is important in the context of the Web where the number of potential sources for a given query is very large. However, this may not be enough and more optimization would be necessary. One technique (Hermes) bases its optimization on caching statistics about sources calls to estimate the cost of possible execution plans. It also uses a notion of expression invariants to derive equivalent execution query plans. The use of cache may not be sufficient for optimization purpose. It could be used in addition to other optimization techniques.

There is also a trend to use adaptive or dynamic approaches in dealing with query optimization. This is motivated by the intrinsic dynamics of the Web where unpredictable events may occur during the execution of a query. The types of actions that are considered in these approaches fall into one of the following cases: (1) change the query execution plan, (2) change the scheduling of operations in the same query execution plan or in different concurrent query plans, (3) introduce new operators to cater for the unpredictable events, or (4) modify the order of inputs of binary operators. Adaptive techniques have yet to demonstrate their applicability to real Web-based applications with large numbers of information sources. There is also a need to show how they react under heavy fluctuations.

Another interesting direction in optimizing queries over Web data integration systems is the use of information quality. The main motivation is that those quality parameters reflect the user's needs better in such environments. One of the approaches (HiQIQ) uses different classes of quality criteria to select relevant sources and rank alternative query plans. The other approach (ObjectGlobe) allows users to specify quality constraints on the execution of queries. These constraints may relate to the expected results, cost of the query, or time for the first results or complete execution. These quality of service (QoS) constraints are then enforced during the execution of the query. Quality constraints are of crucial importance for some applications. A major issue is how to get related information from sources scattered on the Web. Furthermore, due to the "subjective" nature of some of these constraints, the query optimizer may not always succeed in finding the best plans.

An important issue in processing queries over Web data integration systems is to deal with the often limited query capabilities of sources. These limitations have a direct impact on the optimization process. Some query execution plans may be optimal but not feasible. The different query planning strategies focus generally on finding feasible and optimal subgoal orderings based on available bindings and supported conditions at the information sources. Proposed techniques assume a full knowledge of the query capabilities of every participating source. They rely heavily on the way that information sources are described (e.g., binding patterns and free grammars) and the objective function of the optimizer (e.g., number of sources, response time). Using the same source description model may not always be possible across a large spectrum of information sources.

6.2 Web services Querying and Optimization

There are four major research efforts that are related to our proposed approach for querying Web services: Web service discovery, integrating Web services and XML querying, Web services composition, and query optimization over database integration systems.

Web service discovery concerns mainly the location of single Web services either found on thew Web or published in service registries. In our approach, service discovery is only one of the steps in the query process. The goal is to answer declarative and complex queries by combining operations of located Web services. In the following, we review a number of related research efforts that have some overlapping with the query infrastructure we are proposing.

6.2.1 Active XML

Active XML (AXML) [2] enables querying XML documents based on Web services. AXML documents are defined as XML documents where portions correspond to Web service operation invocations. These invocations could be defined explicitly or declaratively as XQuery queries over AXML documents. AXML focuses on different issues related to the evaluation of Web service invocations within an AXML document [66]. These include activation time determination, invocation's arguments discovery, output validity over time, etc. Different techniques drawn from databases and XML research are proposed to address these issues. The authors have also looked at distribution and replication issues for AXML documents [3]. A major difference with our work is that we view Web services as first class objects while Active XML uses Web services as a mean to "update" XML documents. The object of querying in AXML is the XML documents themselves. Additionally, AXML does not support QoWS or any type of optimization in selecting Web services.

6.2.2 Quality-based Optimization in Self-Serv

In [99], the authors propose a technique based on linear programming to optimize service composition. This work is part of the Self-Serv prototype for service composition [16]. The optimization is based on several *QoWS* criteria (e.g., duration, price, reliability). Composite services are represented as a state-chart where a task could be matched to several Web services belonging to the same community. A community is a collection of Web services offering the same functionality but eventually differing in terms of *QoWS*. The authors expressed the optimization problem of finding the best Web services to execute a composite service in the form of a linear programming problem. The constraints being considered are only those introduced by the computation of the *QoWS* of the composite service plan. This work does not take into account global constraints imposed by the application like the existence of partnerships between Web services. The optimization does not consider discount relationships on *QoWS* that may increase the overall quality of the composite service. In addition, pre- and post-operations and post-conditions are not mentioned in that work.

6.2.3 XSRL - A Request Language for Web-Services

In [5], the authors propose a Web service request language (XSRL) based on XML and AI planning techniques. They proposed also a framework to handle and execute XSRL requests. The aim is to provide planning actions under uncertainty on the basis of refinement and revision as new service-related information is acquired (via interaction with the user or UDDI) and as the execution context change. The focus is on defining a language specification for requests for Web services. This includes specifying the core entities of the request and user's scheduling preferences and dependencies among requested Web services. the language is based on XQuery. XSRL requests are translated to generic plans based on AI planning techniques. The plan executor produces then instantiated plans by interacting with UDDI, users, and Web services. This work has some overlapping with our query infrastructure, especially the planing part. However, it is not clear, from the available literature, how the global planning is conducted. The authors gave no details on how a generic plan is obtained. Furthermore *QoWS* and efficiency issues are not addressed.

6.2.4 Data Centric Web Service Optimization

In [88], the authors addressed query optimization for Select-Project-Join queries spanning multiple web services. Targeted applications coordinate data obtained from multiple web services via SQL-like queries. They propose an algorithm to compose web service operations into a pipelined execution plan. Their idea of optimization is based on exploiting parallelism among Web services to minimize the query's total running time. They consider both the case where some precedence constraints, amongst Web services, are present or not. Another problem addressed by this approach is deciding the optimal size of the data that should be sent by a Web service at once, in contrast to sending one tuple at a time. This book addresses a different, yet important, data centric query optimization problem over Web services.

6.2.5 Algebra for Web Services Querying

The work presented in [98] focuses on the theoretical foundation of Web service optimization. It presents a query algebra that supports optimized access to Web services through service-oriented queries. The service query algebra is defined based on a formal service model that provides a high level abstraction of Web services across an application domain. The algebra defines a set of algebraic operators. Algebraic service queries can be formulated using these operators. The authors implemented all of these algebraic operators and presented optimization techniques based on Dynamic Programming.

6.2.6 Multi-Domain Queries over Web Services

Brag et al. [31] addressed the problem of multi-domain queries where each part of the query needs to be answered from a different domains (e.g., seaside locations, flights, publications) by invoking some Web services. They first introduce a theoretical formalism to express such queries. Web services are classified as either exact services, i.e., they have a relational behavior and return a set of unranked answers or search services, i.e, they return a ranked list of answers. They process queries into relational physical access plans that schedule the invocations of Web services and the composition of their input and output. They also address optimization which aims to minimize a cost function in order to obtain the best k answers. The cost model includes the response time of a give query as well as a sum cost metric which corresponds to the cost of producing k answers. Each operator used in the plan will have a cost that can be the cost of computing joins or some monetary cost of using the Web service.

6.2.7 Quality of Web Services

Although the concept of quality of service (QoS) has been mainly used in networking and multimedia applications, there has been recently a surge in adapting this concept to Web services [94]. This required the definition of parameters specific to the Web service environment. how these parameters are specified

Our work presents two interesting directions in treating *QoWS* in the context of Web services. First, we propose a taxonomy for *QoWS* parameters that takes into account several facets of Web service behavior in delivering their functionalities. Second, we present a monitoring scheme that we believe is necessary to sustain the effective use of *QoWS* in any context where efficiency is at stake.

6.2.8 Service Composition

A key difference between the service query model and service composition [62] is that we do not intend to build new Web services that would outsource their functionalities from existing ones. Our goal is to provide query facilities over Web services. Users and applications get information by submitting queries that are resolved by combining access to different Web services. We should note that there is currently a sustained effort to define standards for the specification of Web service orchestration. This includes WSFL (Web Services Flow Language), XLANG, and BPEL4WS (Business Process Execution Language for Web Services).

WSFL [54] uses the notions of flow and global model to define composite services. The flow model relates to the execution sequence of component services. It is defined by a directed graph. Each node, or activity, models a single step of the overall business goal to be achieved. Activities are linked to services through a locator element. This binding can be either static or dynamic. WSFL uses two types of edges to connect activities: control links and data links. Control links define the execution order of the activities. Data links represent the flow of information between activities. The global model specifies how component services interact.

XLANG [65] focuses on language constructs to describe behavioral aspects of Web services and combine them to build multi-party business processes. At the intra-service level, XLANG extends WSDL language by adding a behavior element. A behavior defines the list of actions that belong to the service and their execution order. XLANG defines two types of actions: regular WSDL operations and XLANG-specific actions (e.g., timeout operations). At the inter-service level, XLANG defines a contract element for interconnecting several XLANG service descriptions. The execution order of XLANG actions is defined through control processes (e.g., sequence, while).

BPEL4WS [14] combines the features of both WSFL (support for graph oriented processes) and XLANG (structural constructs for processes) for defining business processes. A business process is composed of several steps called activities. BPEL4WS defines a collection of primitive activities like invoking an operation. These primitive activities are combined into more complex primitives using structural activities provided in BPEL4WS. These include the ability to: (1) define an ordered sequence of steps (sequence); (2) have branching using the "case-statement" approach (switch); (3) define a loop (while); (4) execute one of several alternative paths (pick); and (5) indicate that a collection of steps should be executed in parallel (flow).

These specifications have little or no support for optimization based on *QoWS*. Interestingly, they could be used to generate a detailed description of the service execution plan once it is produced by our optimizer. We could then take advantage of any new technology that supports those specifications.

6.2.9 Optimization in Web Databases and Web Services

Database integration has been subject to a sustained research effort [75]. Query optimization in this context is still a major challenge. A fundamental difference between database query optimization and our approach lies in the manipulated objects. The first class objects in our approach are *services* while *data* is the first class object in databases. In our approach, optimization focuses on *QoWS* parameters related to the behavior of the Web services while in most existing techniques, optimization concerns only the response time of the query execution plan.

Efficiently ordering Web services operations in the service execution plan has some similarities with the classical problem of processing queries over sources with limited capabilities [75]. However, there are several differences with the classical problem found in databases. First, operations need to be discovered and matched against virtual operations. The service execution plan should bear not on virtual operations but on located concrete operations. Second, for any virtual operation, there may be several choices of concrete operations which complicates more query processing and optimization. Finally, our matching strategy allows certain types of matching that may change the binding requirements from those of the corresponding virtual operations.

Chapter 7
Conclusions, Open Issues, and Future Directions

This book addresses key issues to enable efficient access to Web databases and Web services. We described a distributed ontology that allows a meaningful organization of and efficient access to Web databases. We also presented a comprehensive query infrastructure for the emerging concept of Web services. The core of this query infrastructure relates to the efficient delivery of Web services based on the concept of *Quality of Web Service*.

Treating Web services as first class objects is a fundamental step towards achieving the envisioned Semantic Web. Semantics-aware processing of information requires intensive use of Web services. In our research, we propose a new query model where queries are resolved by combining Web service invocations. To efficiently deploy such scheme, we propose an optimization strategy based on aggregating Quality of Web service (*QoWS*) of different Web services. *QoWS* is adjusted through a dynamic rating scheme and multilevel matching. Web service ratings provide an assessment of their behavior. The multilevel matching allows a larger solution space by enabling similar and partial answers.

In the distributed ontology based framework, Web databases are organized and segmented based on simple ontologies that describe coherent slices of the information space. Distributed ontologies of Web databases are established through a simple domain ontology. Inter-ontology relationships are dynamically established between ontologies. In addition, intra-ontology relationships between Web databases are considered. This allows a more flexible and precise querying within an ontology. These relationships form a hierarchy of classes (an information type based classification hierarchy) inside an ontology.

Querying Web services is enabled through a novel three-level query model that provides an easy way for developers to represent the service space and for users to formulate and submit queries. Users formulate declarative queries using relations from the top level (query level). These queries are first transformed to bear on virtual operations defined at the second level. The link between the two first levels is defined through simple mapping rules. Relations, virtual operations, and mapping rules define a schema through which the actual service space is accessed. At a final stage, virtual operations in a given query are dynamically matched to concrete operations leading to a service execution plan that accesses actual Web services. The virtual operations play a central role in the proposed three-level query model. They allow to achieve two important objectives: having generic operations that would be matched in several ways to concrete operations (as explained in the matching scheme that we define) and being able to select an appropriate concrete operation based on non functional properties (*QoWS*). This is of prime importance for the ever expanding service Web. In addition, instead of trying to only find exact match for a query, we propose a more flexible matching scheme where some details of selected Web services differ from what is specified in the request. This has resulted in defining a dynamic multi-level matching scheme between virtual and concrete operations.

The widespread deployment of Web services will result in a fierce competition amongst them. To address this important issue, we designed a complex *QoWS* model to discriminate between competing Web services offering similar functionalities. Examples of *QoWS* includes usage fee and latency. The concept of *QoWS* captures users and applications' requirements for efficiency and hence for query optimization on the Web. In our approach, *QoWS* encompasses a number of quantitative and qualitative parameters that measure the Web service performance in delivering its functionalities [74, 73, 76]. As we are heading towards the semantic Web, "*software agents*" and not humans would be in charge of formulating queries and submitting them on behalf of humans. In such scenario, it is important to consider every aspect of *QoWS* that may influence the resolution of the query.

QoWS parameters may be subject to various fluctuation during a Web service's life time. We addressed this important issue through a monitoring scheme that assesses *QoWS* advertised by service providers based on their actual behavior. Monitoring Web services behavior is important in either calculating *QoWS* parameters values or assessing a Web services claim in terms of promised *QoWS*. Our monitoring *rates* the behavior of Web services in delivering their functionalities in terms of every *QoWS* parameter. This is conducted by collecting different information on the Web services and computing the *QoWS* distance metric.

Selecting an optimal service execution plan is key to the successful deployment of our query infrastructure over Web services. We addressed this challenging endeavor, exacerbated by the large number of competing Web services, by first devising a cost model based on *QoWS* and then proposing several optimization techniques. These techniques differ in the way they make their decisions and the constraints they consider. We especially focused on two important constraints: binding requirements inherent to the proper invocation of Web service operations and discount relationships that may exist between two partners.

Open Issues

There are several interesting extensions that can be considered for our query infrastructure. One of them is to develop semantic-based optimization techniques for Web services. This would require to use "intelligent" agents that may take advantage of the current context (e.g., semantic of application) to enhance optimization. Another extension is to cater for the dynamic and volatile nature of Web services. Adaptive techniques need to be designed to compensate the effects on the service execution plan efficiency of unpredictable events during run time. For example, a Web service may become unavailable and needs to be replaced by a Web service offering similar functionalities. The replacement strategy should not decrease the overall quality of the service execution plan.

Future Research

Future research, along the philosophy of this book, focuses on supporting the strong synergy between data and services on the Semantic Web. This mainly concerns research on data and service integration on the Semantic Web. A special emphasize would be on devising novel query paradigms and original strategies for efficiently delivering Web services and Web databases in an integrated way. Other avenues for this research concerns query processing and optimization techniques for data streaming and Grids based on Web services. One assumption that we made in this book is that Web services are invoked through a single operation model in which operations are independent from each other. An interesting research direction is to assume that interactions between the client and the Web service are conversational and long-running. In this particular case, a service execution plan will have to take into account the conversational nature of the Web services and hence introduce more constraints. Querying mashups [17] and integrating linked data [20] are two other avenues where our distributed ontologies and web service query model can be useful and are worth pursuing.

Going beyond Web services as strictly defined in this book is another direction of interest. The idea is to consider other form of service-like interactions on the Web including mashups and API. Indeed there have been a widespread use of this technologies as a fast and easy way to consume and combine data from different sources. In addition, many online resources publish well defined APIs, like Google Apps APIs, for easy integration in Web applications. The concept of querying as introduced in this book can be then extended to those APIs. Challenges include dealing with different types of data like maps and voice and being able to handle large amount of data produced by using these APIs.

References

1. E. Aarts and J. Korst. *Simulated Annealing and Boltzman Machines: : A Stochastic Approach to Combinatorial Optimization and Neural Computing*. John Wiley and Sons, New York, USA, January 1989.
2. S. Abiteboul, O. Benjelloun, and T. Milo. Web Services and Data Integration. In *International Conference on Web Information Systems Engineering*, pages 3–6, Singapore, December 2002.
3. S. Abiteboul, A. Bonifati, G. Cobena, I. Manolescu, and T. Milo. Dynamic XML Documents with Distribution and Replication. In *Proceedings of the ACM SIGMOD International Conference on Management of Data*, pages 527–538, San Diego, California, USA, June 2003.
4. S. Adali, K. S. Candan, Y. Papakonstantinou, and V. S. Subrahmanian. Query Caching and Optimization in Distributed Mediator Systems. In *Proceedings of the ACM SIGMOD International Conference on Management of Data*, pages 137–148, Montreal, Canada, June 1996.
5. M. Aiello, M. P. Papazoglou, M. Carman J. Yang, M. Pistore, L. Serafini, and P. Traverso. A Request Language for Web-Services Based on Planning and Constraint Satisfaction. In *Proceedings of the 3rd International Workshop on Technologies for E-Services*, pages 76–85, Hong Kong, China, August 2002.
6. B. Amann, C. Beeri, I. Fundulaki, and M. Scholl. Querying XML Sources Using an Ontology-based Mediator. In *Proceedings of the 10th International Conference on Cooperative Information Systems*, pages 429–448, Irvine, California, USA, October 2002.
7. J. L. Ambite and C. A. Knoblock. Flexible and Scalable Query Planning in Distributed and Heterogeneous Environments. In *Proceedings of the 4th International Conference on Artificial Intelligence Planning Systems*, pages 3–10, Pittsburgh, Pennsylvania, USA, June 1998.
8. L. Amsaleg, P. Bonnet, M. J. Franklin, A. Tomasic, and T. Urhan. Improving Responsiveness for Wide-Area Data Access. *IEEE Data Engineering Bulletin*, 20(3):3–11, September 1997.
9. G. O. Arocena and A. O. Mendelzon. WebOQL: Restructuring Documents, Databases and Webs. In *Proceedings of the 14th International Conference on Data Engineering*, pages 24–33, Orlando, Florida, USA, February 1998.
10. R. H. Arpaci-Dusseau, E. Anderson, N. Treuhaft, D. E. Culler, J. M. Hellerstein, D. Patterson, and K. Yelick. Cluster I/O with River: Making the Fast Case Common. In *Proceedings of the 6th Workshop on I/O in Parallel and Distributed Systems*, pages 10–22, Atlanta, Georgia, USA, May 1999.
11. R. Avnur and J. Hellerstein. Eddies: Continuously Adaptive Query Processing. In *Proceedings of the ACM SIGMOD International Conference on Management of Data*, pages 261–272, Dallas, Texas, USA, May 2000.
12. S. Baker, V. Cahill, and P. Nixon. Using Bridging Boundaries: CORBA in Perspective. *IEEE Internet Computing*, 1(3):43–57, May 1997.

13. C. Batini, M. Lenzerini, and S. B. Navathe. A Comparative Analysis of Methodologies for Database Schema Integration. *ACM Computing Surveys*, 18(4):324–364, December 1986.

14. BEA, IBM, and Microsoft. *Business Process Execution Language for Web Services (BPEL4WS)*. http://xml.coverpages.org/bpel4ws.html, 2003.

15. B. Benatallah, A. Bouguettaya, and A. Elmagarmid. *An Overview of Multidatabase Systems: Past and Present*, chapter 1. Morgan Kaufmann, San Francisco, California, USA, January 1999.

16. B. Benatallah, Q. Z. Sheng, A. H. H. Ngu, and M. Dumas. Declarative Composition and Peer-to-Peer Provisioning of Dynamic Web Services. In *Proceedings of the 18th International Conference on Data Engineering*, pages 297–308, San Jose, California, USA, February 2002.

17. Djamal Benslimane, Schahram Dustdar, and Amit P. Sheth. Services mashups: The new generation of web applications. *IEEE Internet Computing*, 12(5):13–15, 2008.

18. T. Berners-Lee. *Services and Semantics: Web Architecture*. http://www.w3.org/2001/04/30-tbl, 2001.

19. T. Berners-Lee, J. Hendler, and O. Lassila. The Semantic Web. *Scientific American*, 284(5):34–43, May 2001.

20. Tim Berners-Lee. Linked data. *International Journal on Semantic Web and Information Systems*, 4(2):1, 2006.

21. L. Bouganim, F. Fabret, C. Mohan, and P. Valduriez. Dynamic Query Scheduling in Data Integration Systems. In *Proceedings of the 16th International Conference on Data Engineering*, pages 425–434, San Diego, California, USA, February/March 2000.

22. A. Bouguettaya. Large Multidatabases: Beyond Federation and Global Schema Integration. In *Proceedings of the 5th Australasian Database Conference*, pages 258–273, Christchurch, New Zealand, January 1994.

23. A. Bouguettaya, B. Benatallah, and A. Elmagarmid. *Interconnecting Heterogeneous Information Systems*. Kluwer Academic Publishers, Boston, USA, August 1998.

24. A. Bouguettaya, B. Benatallah, L. Hendra, M. Ouzzani, and J. Beard. Supporting Dynamic Interactions Among Web-Based Information Sources. *IEEE Transactions on Knowledge and Data Engineering*, 12(5):779–801, September/October 2000.

25. A. Bouguettaya, B. Benatallah, M. Ouzzani, and L. Hendra. Using Java and CORBA for Implementing Internet Databases. In *Proceedings of the 15th International Conference on Data Engineering*, pages 218–227, Sydney, Australia, March 1999.

26. A. Bouguettaya, B. Benatallah, M. Ouzzani, and L. Hendra. WebFINDIT - An Architecture and System for Querying Web Databases. *IEEE Internet Computing*, 3(4):30–41, July/August 1999.

27. A. Bouguettaya, A. K. Elmagarmid, B. Medjahed, and M. Ouzzani. Ontology-based Support for Digital Government. In *Proceedings of 27th International Conference on Very Large Data Bases*, pages 633–636, Roma, Italy, September 2001.

28. A. Bouguettaya and R. King. Large multidatabases: Issues and directions. In *IFIP DS-5 Semantics of Interoperable Database Systems (Editor s: D. K. Hsiao, E. J. Neuhold, and R. Sacks-Davis)*. Elsevier Publishers, 1993.

29. A. Bouguettaya, B. Medjahed, A. Rezgui, M. Ouzzani, and Z. Wen. Privacy Preserving Composition of Government Web Services (Demo Paper). In *Proceedings of the 2002 National Conference on Digital Government Research*, pages 429–432, Los Angeles, California, USA, May 2002.

30. A. Bouguettaya, M. Ouzzani, B. Medjahed, and J. Cameron. Managing Government Databases. *IEEE Computer*, 34(2):56–64, February 2001.

31. Daniele Braga, Stefano Ceri, Florian Daniel, and Davide Martinenghi. Optimization of multi-domain queries on the web. *PVLDB*, 1(1):562–573, 2008.

32. R. Braumandl, M. Keidl, A. Kemper, D. Kossmann, A. Kreutz, S. Seltzsam, and K. Stocker. ObjectGlobe: Ubiquitous Query Processing on the Internet. *The VLDB Journal*, 10(1):48–71, June 2001.

33. C. Bussler, D. Fensel, and A. Maedche. A conceptual architecture for semantic Web enabled Web services. *SIGMOD Record*, 31(4), 2002.

34. F. Casati, D. Georgakopoulos, and M.-C. Shan, editors. *2nd International Workshop on Technologies for E-Services*, LNCS 2193, September 2001.
35. The World Wide Web Consortium. *Service Description.* http://www.w3.org/standards/webofservices/description.
36. The World Wide Web Consortium. *Simple Object Access Protocol (SOAP).* http://www.w3.org/standards/techs/soap.
37. M. Conti, M. Kumar, S. K. Das, and B. A. Shirazi. Quality of Service Issues in Internet Web Services. *IEEE Transactions on Computers*, 51(6):593–594, June 2002.
38. W. Du, R. Krishnamurthy, and M.-C. Shan. Query Optimization in a Heterogeneous DBMS. In *Proceedings of the 18th International Conference on Very Large Data Bases*, pages 277–291, Vancouver, Canada, August 1992.
39. O. M. Duschka. *Query Planning and Optimization in Information Integration*. PhD thesis, Computer Science Department, Stanford University, Stanford, California, December 1997.
40. O. M. Duschka and M. R. Genesereth. Query Planning in Infomaster. In *Proceedings of the 12th Annual ACM Symposium on Applied Computing*, pages 109–111, San Jose, California, USA, February 1997.
41. E. Evans and D. Rogers. Using Java Applets and CORBA for Multi-User Distributed Applications. *IEEE Internet Computing*, 1(5):52–57, September 1997.
42. D. Fensel, H. Lausen, A. Polleres, J. de Bruijn, M. Stollberg, D. Roman, and J. Domingue. *Enabling semantic web services: the web service modeling ontology*. Springer, 2007.
43. D. Florescu, A. Levy, I. Manolescu, and D. Suciu. Query Optimization in the Presence of Limited Access Patterns. In *Proceedings of the ACM SIGMOD International Conference on Management of Data*, pages 311–322, Philadelphia, Pennsylvania, USA, June 1999.
44. H. Garcia-Molina, W. Labio, and R. Yerneni. Capability Sensitive Query Processing on Internet Sources. In *Proceedings of the 15th International Conference on Data Engineering*, pages 50–59, Sydney, Australia, March 1999.
45. H. Garcia-Molina, Y. Papakonstantinou, D. Quass, A. Rajaraman, Y. Sagiv, J. D. Ullman, V. Vassalos, and J. Widom. The TSIMMIS Approach to Mediation: Data Models and Languages. *Journal of Intelligent Information Systems*, 8(2):117–132, 1997.
46. G. Gardarin, F. Sha, and Z. Tang. Calibrating the Query Optimizer Cost Model of IRO-DB. In *Proceedings of the 22nd International Conference on Very Large Data Bases*, pages 378–389, Bombay, India, September 1996.
47. G. Graefe. Query Evaluation Techniques for Large Databases. *ACM computing Survey*, 25(2):73–170, June 1993.
48. L. Gravano and Y. Papakonstantinou. Mediating and Metasearching on the Internet. *IEEE Data Engineering Bulletin*, 21(2):28–36, June 1998.
49. L. M. Haas, D. Kossmann, E. L. Wimmers, and J. Yang. Optimizing Queries across Diverse Data Sources. In *Proceedings of the 23rd International Conference on Very Large Data Bases*, pages 276–285, Athens, Greece, August 1997.
50. D. Heimbigner and D. McLeod. A Federated Architecture for Information Systems. *ACM Transactions on Office Information Systems*, 3(3):253–278, July 1985.
51. J. M. Hellerstein, M. J. Franklin, S. Chandrasekaran, A. Deshpande, K. Hildrum, S. Madden, V. Ramana, and M. A. Shah. Adaptive Query Processing: Technology in Evolution. *IEEE Data Engineering Bulletin*, 23(2):7–18, June 2000.
52. I. Horrocks. DAML+OIL: a Description Logic for the Semantic Web. *IEEE Data Engineering Bulletin*, 25(1):4–9, March 2002.
53. A. R. Hurson, M. W. Bright, and H. Pakzad. *Multidatabase Systems: An Advanced Solution for Global Information Sharing*. IEEE Computer Society Press, Los Alamitos, California, USA, 1994.
54. IBM. *Web Services Flow Language (WSFL)*. http://xml.coverpages.org/wsfl.html, 2003.
55. Z. Ives, D. Florescu, M. Friedman, A. Levy, and D. Weld. An Adaptive Query Execution System for Data Integration. In *Proceedings of the ACM SIGMOD International Conference on Management of Data*, pages 299–310, Philadelphia, PA, USA, June 1999.

56. D. Konopnicki and O. Shmueli. WWW Information Gathering : The W3QL Query Language and the W3QS System. *ACM Transaction on Database Systems*, 23(4):369–410, December 1998.

57. A. Levy, A. Rajaraman, and J. Ordille. Querying Heterogeneous Information Sources using Source Descriptions. In *Proceedings of the 22nd International Conference on Very Large Data Bases*, Bombay, India, 1996.

58. R. MacGregor. A Deductive Pattern Matcher. In *Proceedings of AAAI-88, The National Conference on Artificial Intelligence*, pages 403–408, St. Paul, Minnesota, USA, August 1988.

59. B. Medjahed, A. Bouguettaya, and A. Elmagarmid. Composing Web Services on the Semantic Web. *The VLDB Journal*, 12(4):333–351, November 2003.

60. B. Medjahed, A. Bouguettaya, and M. Ouzzani. Semantic Web Enabled E-Government Services. In *Proceedings of the 2003 National Conference on Digital Government Research*, pages 237–240, Boston, Massachusetts, USA, May 2003.

61. B. Medjahed, M. Ouzzani, and A. Bouguettaya. Using Web Services in E-Government Applications. In *Proceedings of the 2002 National Sciences Foundation Conference on Digital Government Research*, pages 371–376, Los Angeles, California, USA, May 2002.

62. B. Medjahed, A. Rezgui, A. Bouguettaya, and M. Ouzzani. Infrastructure for E-Government Web Services. *IEEE Internet Computing*, 7(1):56–64, January/February 2003.

63. E. Mena, A. Illarramendi, V. Kashyap, and A. Sheth. OBSERVER: An Approach for Query Processing in Global Information Systems based on Interoperation across Pre-existing Ontologies. *International Journal Distributed and Parallel Databases*, 8(2):223–271, April 2000.

64. A. O. Mendelzon, G. A. Mihaila, and T. Milo. Querying the World Wide Web. *International Journal on Digital Libraries*, 1(1):54–67, April 1997.

65. Microsoft. *Web Services for Business Process Design (XLANG)*. http://xml.coverpages.org/xlang.html, 2003.

66. T. Milo, S. Abiteboul, B. Amann, O. Benjelloun, and F. Dang Ngoc. Exchanging Intensional XML Data. In *Proceedings of the ACM SIGMOD International Conference on Management of Data*, pages 289–300, San Diego, California, USA, June 2003.

67. H. Naacke, G. Gardarin, and A. Tomasic. Leveraging Mediator Cost Models with Heterogeneous Data Sources. In *Proceedings of the 14th International Conference on Data Engineering*, pages 351–360, Orlando, Florida, February 1998.

68. F. Naumann. Data Fusion and Data Quality. In *Proceedings of the New Techniques and Technologies for Statistics Seminar*, pages 147–154, Sorrento, Italy, May 1998.

69. F. Naumann and U. Lesser. Quality–driven Integration of Heterogeneous Information Systems. In *Proceedings of the 25st International Conference on Very Large Data Bases*, pages 447–458, Edinburgh, UK, September 1999.

70. M. Nodine, W. Bohrer, and A. H. H. Ngu. Semantic Brokering over Dynamic Heterogeneous Data Sources in InfoSleuth. In *Proceedings of the 15th International Conference on Data Engineering*, pages 358–365, Sydney, Australia, March 1999.

71. R. Orfali and D. Harkey. *Client/Server Programming with Java and CORBA*. John Wiley & Sons, Inc., New York, USA, 1997.

72. M. Ouzzani, B. Benatallah, and A. Bouguettaya. Ontological Approach for Information Discovery in Internet Databases. *Distributed and Parallel Databases, an International Journal*, 8(3):367–392, July 2000.

73. M. Ouzzani and A. Bouguettaya. A Query Paradigm for Web Services. In *Proceedings of the 1st International Conference on Web Services*, pages 152–155, Las Vegas, NV, USA, June 2003.

74. M. Ouzzani and A. Bouguettaya. Efficient Access to Web Services. *IEEE Internet Computing*, 8(2):34–44, March/April 2004.

75. M. Ouzzani and A. Bouguettaya. Query Processing and Optimization on the Web. *Distributed and Parallel Databases, an International Journal*, 15(3):187–218, May 2004.

76. M. Ouzzani, A. Bouguettaya, and B. Medjahed. Optimized Querying of E-Government Services. In *Proceedings of the 2003 National Conference on Digital Government Research*, pages 363–366, Boston, Massachusetts, USA, May 2003.

77. F. Ozcan, S. Nural, P. Koskal, C. Evrendilek, and A. Dogac. Dynamic Query Optimization in Multidatabases. *IEEE Data Engineering Bulletin*, 20(3):38–45, September 1997.

78. M. Tamer Ozsu and Patrick Valduriez. *Principles of Distributed Database Systems*. Prentice Hall, New Jersey, USA, 1999.

79. A. Rezgui, A. Bouguettaya, and Z. Malik. A Reputation-based Approach to Preserving Privacy in Web Services. In *Proceedings of the 4th International Workshop on Technologies for E-Services*, pages 91–103, Berlin, Germany, September 2003.

80. A. Rezgui, M. Ouzzani, A. Bouguettaya, and B. Medjahed. Preserving Privacy in Web Services. In *Proceedings of the 4th International ACM Workshop on Web Information and Data Management*, pages 56–62, November 2002.

81. M. T. Roth, F. Ozcan, and L. M. Haas. Cost Models DO Matter: Providing Cost Information for Diverse Data Sources in a Federated System. In *Proceedings of the 25th International Conference on Very Large Data Bases*, pages 599–610, Edinburgh, Scotland, UK, September 1999.

82. M. T. Roth and P. Schwarz. Don't Scrap It, Wrap It! A Wrapper Architecture for Legacy Data Sources. In *Proceedings of the 23rd International Conference on Very Large Data Bases*, pages 266–275, Athens, Greece, August 1997.

83. A. Ruiz, R. Corchuelo and. Duran, and M. Toro. Automated Support for Quality Requirements in Web-Based Systems. In *Proceedings of the 8th IEEE Workshop on Future Trends of Distributed Computing Systems*, pages 48–55, Bologna, Italy, October-November 2001.

84. P. Selinger, M. Astrahan, D. Chamberlin, R. Lorie, and T. Price. Access Path Selection in a Relational Database Management System. In *Proceedings of the ACM SIGMOD International Conference on Management of Data*, pages 23–34, Boston, Massachusetts, May/June 1979.

85. M.-C. Shan. Pegasus Architecture and Design Principles. In *Proceedings of the ACM SIGMOD International Conference on Management of Data*, pages 422–425, Washington DC, USA, June 1993.

86. Amit P. Sheth and James A. Larson. Federated Database Systems and Managing Distributed, Heterogeneous, and Autonomous Databases. *ACM Computing Surveys*, 22(3):183–226, September 1990.

87. S. Spaccapietra and C. Parent. A Step Forward in Solving Structural Conflicts. *IEEE Transactions on Knowledge and Data Engineering*, 6(2):258–274, April 1994.

88. Utkarsh Srivastava, Kamesh Munagala, Jennifer Widom, and Rajeev Motwani. Query optimization over web services. In Umeshwar Dayal, Kyu-Young Whang, David B. Lomet, Gustavo Alonso, Guy M. Lohman, Martin L. Kersten, Sang Kyun Cha, and Young-Kuk Kim, editors, *VLDB*, pages 355–366. ACM, 2006.

89. A. S. Tannenbaum and M. van Steen. *Distributed Systems: Principles and Paradigms*. Prentice Hall, New Jersey, USA, 2002.

90. A. Tomasic, L. Rashid, and P. Valduriez. Scaling Heterogeneous Database and Design of DISCO. In *Proceedings of the 16th International Conference on Distributing Computing systems*, pages 449–457, Hong Kong, China, May 1996.

91. S. Tsur, S. Abiteboul, R. Agrawal, U. Dayal, J. Klein, and G. Weikum. Are Web Services the Next Revolution in e-Commerce? (Panel). In *Proceedings of the 27th International Conference on Very Large Data Bases*, pages 633–636, Roma, Italy, September 2001.

92. UDDI. *Universal Description, Discovery, and Integration*. http://www.uddi.org.

93. International Telecommunication Union. *ITU-T Recommendation E.800: Terms and Definitions Related to Quality of Service and Network Performance Including Dependability, ITU-T*, 1994.

94. S. Vinoski. Service Discovery 101. *IEEE Internet Computing*, 7(1):69–71, January/February 2003.

95. G. Wiederhold. Mediators in the Architecture of Future Information Systems. *IEEE Computer*, 25(3):38–49, 1992.

96. Y. Yerneni, C. Li, J. D. Ullman, and H. Garcia-Molina. Optimizing Large Join Queries in Mediation Systems. In *Proceedings of the International Conference Database Theory*, pages 348–364, Jerusalem, January 1999.

97. K. Yoon and C. Hwang. *Multiple Attribute Decision Making: An Introduction*. Thousand Oaks: Sage, Thousand Oaks, California, USA, January 1995.

98. Qi Yu and Athman Bouguettaya. Framework for web service query algebra and optimization. *TWEB*, 2(1), 2008.

99. L. Zeng, B. Benatallah, M. Dumas, J. Kalagnanam, and Q. Z. Sheng. Quality Driven Web Services Composition. In *Proceedings of the 12th international conference on World Wide Web*, pages 411–421, Budapest, Hungary, May 2003.

100. Q. Zhu and P. Larson. Global Query Processing and Optimization in the CORDS Multi-database System. In *Proceedings of International Conference on Parallel and Distributed Computing Systems*, pages 640–646, Dijon, France, September 1996.